INTO THE ENCHANTED FOREST
LANGUAGE, DRAMA AND SCIENCE IN PRIMARY SCHOOLS

EDITED BY AVRIL BROCK

Trentham Books

First published in 1999 by Trentham Books Limited

Trentham Books Limited
Westview House
734 London Road
Oakhill
Stoke on Trent
Staffordshire
England ST4 5NP

British Cataloguing in Publication Data
A catalogue record for this book is available from the
British Library
ISBN 1 85856 132 9
(hb ISBN 1 85856 131 0)

Designed and typeset by Trentham Print Design Ltd., Chester and printed in
Great Britain by Cromwell Press Ltd., Wiltshire.

CONTENTS

LIST OF CONTRIBUTORS

Avril Brock, the research project coordinator, is a Senior Lecturer in Language and the Early Years Coordinator at Bradford College.

All the students involved in the project were B.Ed. (Hons.) Degree students studying language and literature as the major subject of their four year degree programme at Bradford College. Those who worked with children in the Enchanted Forest had selected an elective study module to further their knowledge and experience of children's language development.

Rebecca Adams, Sara Ali, Lakhbir Kaur Bassi and **Nazia Hussain** were fourth year students who formed part of the original research team in 1997, examining children negotiating meanings in collaborative problem-solving situations. Their enthusiasm and total involvement in the project enabled the successful facilitation of the research.

Manorma Dass, Harbans Kaur Gill, Rona Hepton, Noreen Hussain, Baksho Kaur, Claire Nixon, Hilary Rider and **Mohinder Kaur Sandhu** undertook an elective entitled 'The use of drama in developing children's language'. This was a split programme consisting of seminars in college and follow up work in school with groups of children throughout the first school age range.

Rona, Baksho, Claire and Hilary have now all successfully completed their degrees and have teaching jobs. Manorma, Harbans, Noreen and Mohinder are in the final year of their degree programme, having undertaken a part time course alongside working in school as bilingual support assistants.

John Hollingworth is a Senior Lecturer in Primary Science and Post Graduate Course Tutor at Bradford College. He was a member of the research team and planned and organised the science activities and tutored the research team.

Maggie Power was the class teacher and Religious Education coordinator at Grange Road First School and is now a Lecturer in Religious Education and Language at Bradford College. She was the school coordinator in the research team.

The Forest was 'replanted' the following year at All Saints First School in Bradford. The tasks were introduced to Year 3 and Year 4 children at the school by third year students. They were Carol Hannam, Sarah Davies and Lisa Hainsworth, science majors, who really developed the children's understanding of the science involved in the project. Later in the year a group of third year language majors undertook drama and storytelling with children of different age groups in the school.

The children of both schools have contributed to the art work contained in this book. All the children's names have been changed.

FOREWORD

This book begins with a chapter about collaborative problem-solving and indeed the book itself has been my problem which I have solved collaboratively with help from many friends. All the writers of the chapters have collaborated – with each other, with the research team, with the teachers and children of the school.

Many of our colleagues in the Department of Teacher Education have supported us. Our technicians – Ron and Andy – collaborated in the construction of the Forest, Sheeryn and her young daughters collaborated in the transcriptions and translations. Thanks to the language team, to Norah for inspiration, but mainly to Barré, Jean, Keira and Maggie for being critical readers.

The work could not have taken place without all the children participating and the involvement of Grange Road First School. The succeeding project occurred through the invitation and ensuing support by All Saints First School. Many thanks to all staff and children.

My daughter Jackie pushed the book forward after spending many hours revising and editing, sitting at my shoulder in Coxley, reading proofs in Japan.

Even J.J. must be mentioned, he was right in saying there would be tears before bedtime, but not when he kept advising me to throw it in the bin!

But thanks to Tasha most of all, Tasha the secretary cat who kept the computer chair warm, willing inspiration into the blank screen when I wasn't there.

INTRODUCTION

INTO THE ENCHANTED FOREST
A LANGUAGE EXPERIENCE STRATEGY
AVRIL BROCK

anguage, whether first, second or subsequent, is learned in context.
And it is learned through use – talking, listening, reading and writing. This book describes how primary school children learned and developed their language through a project – The Enchanted Forest – in which they worked collaboratively to solve clues and complete tasks, in a constructed make-believe environment.

The book is written by the researchers, teachers and student teachers who set up the project and observed the children as they worked their way through it. Many of the tasks the children were set were science based, so their learning encompassed science as well as language. Because they role-played in this fantasy world, drama was the third curriculum subject covered by the project.

Most of the ideas and activities described came about at Grange Road First School, in an inner city area of Bradford. The school caters for children aged 4 to 8 years old. Most of them were involved in one project or another in the Enchanted Forest. The majority of them are at least bilingual and speak Panjabi as their first language, and English and Urdu as their additional languages. Other languages understood by some of the children are Farsi, Arabic and Hindi. Most of the pupils are Muslim and attend a Madressa after school, where they learn to read the Qur'an.

The class teacher involved in the project, Maggie Power, has initiated and produced professional media videos. She has also collaborated in writing storybooks and resource packs for teachers. In the mid 1980s she took part in Bradford's Storybox Project, working in partnership with professional shadow puppeteers, storytellers, poets, playwrights and dramatists.

The school has a reputation for being innovative in terms of language development, so was an obvious choice for the research project – imaginative and enthusiastic children, a head teacher who allowed her staff to develop ideas, an innovative class teacher who really accomplished dramatic targets. And they had an empty classroom!

The Forest was made available for all the children and teachers in the school and came to be used for whole class drama, music and storytelling sessions. It provided a stimulus for design and technology, for geography and science work. Trainee teachers from Bradford College worked in the Forest with the different age groups. The school welcomed partnership with the college and wholeheartedly supported student involvement.

Teacher training institutions should enhance and accredit students' achievements in school when they undertake and document small scale research projects. Students may have some advantages over practising teachers in that:

- they have to research and write as part of their training

- they are allocated time and opportunity to do the work

- the pressure of normal school timetabling and whole class teaching does not necessarily apply

- the work undertaken may differ from the everyday timetable.

Much of the students' work is of a high quality and teacher trainers and the teaching profession should capitalise on the work achieved. The teacher training agency (TTA) is keen for small scale research projects to be piloted and disseminated to enhance our understanding of how children learn and achieve.

The idea and purpose for the Enchanted Forest stems from a variety of professional experiences and practical observations of children learning. I have always been interested in setting up role-play situations for children and engaging them in drama activities. I believe that children gain understanding of concepts from engaging in first hand experiences. Story, role-play and drama are means of creating such meaningful experiences, in which children can actively participate and reflect upon their learning. This is of particular importance for bilingual children. They not only have to produce English, but they also have to negotiate meanings, communicate competently and develop their understanding of concepts in this additional language. They therefore need contextualised experiences to enable them to use language purposefully. Building on the foundations of these beliefs, I decided to create the Enchanted Forest as a dramatic environment, where children could engage in problem-solving activities, requiring little adult involvement. This, I hoped, would enable the children to think for themselves, negotiating through language.

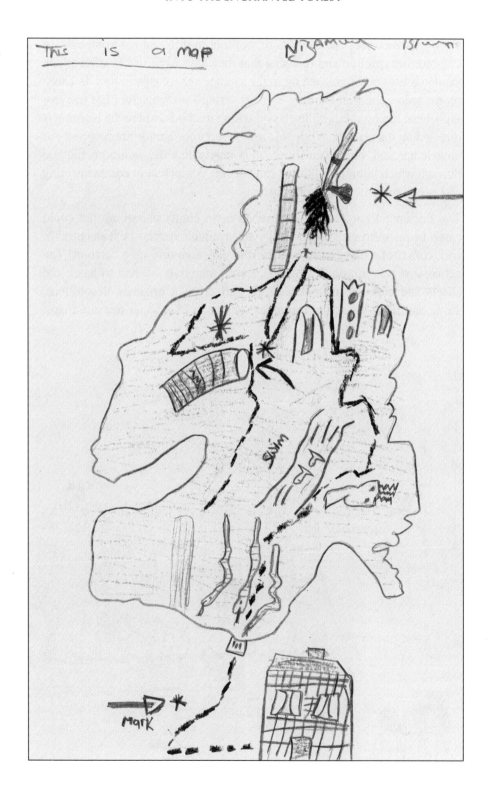

This book describes the benefits of working in different environments, of empowering children and realising that they have expertise to offer which cannot always be capitalised on in the average school curriculum. In classrooms today, children learning by discovering for themselves has increasingly been replaced by whole class teaching methods, where the learning is directed by the teacher. While this may be appropriate for many aspects of knowledge and skill acquisition, it is surely not the optimum method through which bilingual children can become competent in communicating and negotiating meaning in English.

The Enchanted Forest was constructed in an empty classroom but could easily be reconstructed in practically any available space – be it an entrance hall, corner of a classroom, nursery role-play area or even a corridor! The actual cost was minimal. We simply used materials we had to hand: old sheets and curtains, cellophane, foil and crêpe, Christmas decorations, string and rope. We added resources such as masks, paper treasure maps,

old keys and playshapes of trees, animals and a palace made from hardboard.

We managed to build the Forest without any of the children finding out what we were doing. To create a dramatic atmosphere we first darkened the room by swathing it in black paper. The fluorescent light fittings were covered with cellophane to cast a greenish woodland hue. Large green leaves covered the walls and camouflaged green tree trunks were suspended from the ceiling. A giant web complete with spiders hung from the ceiling and creepers, fronds and vines of different textures hung all around. An owl swooped from a painting in front of mysterious distant towers. Different perspectives of sky and nimbus clouds were depicted in a painting on one wall. A synthetic blue river wended its way across the middle of the room from the entrance to its source in a shimmering waterfall. Fishes played in the pool at the bottom of the waterfall and diamonds of silver foil sparkled in among them.

Palm trees, jungle creepers and fruitbearing branches grew all around the Forest, with unusual giraffe-like animals peering from behind. In a cave in the corner of the Forest was a dark secretive grotto, with creepers dangling over the entrance, and bells tinkling in the background, which beckoned the children invitingly. Wooden tree stumps, magic pineapples and mysterious musical chimes all added to the eeriness of the Forest. A low moulded tunnel stretched through the Forest with a carpet of leaves and a velvety darkened boulder in the middle. This had to be manoeuvred if travellers were to get access to the other side. A minareted palace draped in the finest muslin enclosed a shrouded empty throne room.

The writers in this book undertake a variety of activities in the Enchanted Forest with different groups of children throughout the school. Reflecting critically, they describe their initial intentions and their apprehensions, and how they had sometimes to change their practice in response to the children's reactions. The students studied language as a main subject, not drama. Their accounts of their activities should give readers confidence, as well as ideas. They relate their nervousness, their success and the children's enhanced language development. This partnership and collaboration between students, lecturers, teachers and children offered opportunities for the participants to develop as practitioners in creative and non-judgmental situations.

In Chapter 1, Collaborative problem-solving in the Enchanted Forest, I explain how the initial work in the Forest was organised specifically for group work and the negotiation of meaning and show how children were able to be proactive in managing their own learning in the imaginative context and how they collaborated in the problems. The problem-solving activities in the Enchanted Forest created a context for the children to develop English and Science in the National Curriculum (see National Curriculum Appendix 1). The tasks had a focus of underlying scientific concepts and they targeted scientific vocabulary.

In Chapter 2, Developing Science in The Enchanted Forest, John Hollingworth and I explore the nature and purposes of the scientific activities. We discuss the children's conceptual and procedural understanding in science through the Enchanted Forest experience. The potential for the development of children's scientific knowledge and scientific process skills are identified and the learning styles provided in the Enchanted Forest are discussed with regard to their effectiveness in promoting children's learning in science.

In 1997 a core group of four students, Sara Ali, Lakhbir Kaur Bassi, Rebecca Adams and Nazia Hussain, worked on the research project in the Enchanted Forest and analysed how children negotiate meanings and what connotations they have for the language used. Their main aim was to see how children constructed word meaning, and to reflect on how they drew on their own previous knowledge and the experiences of the other children in the groups. Their results are documented in Chapter 3, Children making meaning and negotiating understanding.

In Chapter 4, Supporting Panjabi children's oral culture, I show the importance of supporting bilingual children's language, culture and identity. Nazia and Sara supported their first language through story and the practical activities, then I re-entered the Forest with the children and discovered a wealth of personal oral culture from the children. They were familiar with stories told in their own families and eagerly demonstrated their expertise to a listening adult.

In Chapter 5, Developing children's confidence in speaking in first and second languages through drama, the students relate how their initial sessions were hindered by their own expectations, but how they eventually learned to build on the children's interests to encourage language development in the drama sessions. Hilary Rider and Noreen Hussain aimed primarily to enhance children's bilingual skills. On a personal level, they also wanted to gain more confidence in teaching drama, knowing that drama supported and developed children's imaginations and oral language.

Manorma Dass and Baksho Kaur used the story 'Peter and the Wolf in their quest to develop children's speaking and listening skills by encouraging communication and cooperation with others. Harbans Kaur Gill and Mohinder Kaur Sandhu selected 'Never laugh at bears'. They set out to encourage the children to use their first language and so develop confidence in expressing their thoughts and feelings orally in role-play.

Rona Hepton and Claire Nixon used the Forest's space and opportunities to develop children's physical and mental improvisation in drama and story, evoking emotional and multi-sensory responses. They involved children in oral storytelling and examined the fundamental elements of narrative used by the children. They discuss the concrete experiences which enabled the children to broaden their vocabulary and repertoire and reveal the potential of drama for promoting language development.

In Chapter 6, How storytelling in an imaginative context affects the stories children write, Lakhbir Kaur Bassi investigates whether stories that were told, rather than, read to children would affect how they wrote imaginative stories. Would they adopt ideas from oral storytelling when writing their own stories? Storytelling can provoke a shared response of excitement and anticipation and can help build children's confidence in writing. The Forest provided an imaginative context which enabled Lakhbir to give the children experiences and purposes for writing (see National Curriculum Appendix 1).

In Chapter 7, Partnership and collaboration, Maggie Power discusses the purposes and benefits of partnership undertaken not for assessment but to enable staff and students to work collaboratively, sharing and developing ideas. Maggie is committed to partnership and training. She successfully coordinated the students, staff and children in their work in the Enchanted Forest.

While she was taking a visitor to the school into the Enchanted Forest and explaining about some of their activities, one child remarked –

'I don't know if it is true or not, or whether it is just a very good story.'

CHAPTER 1
COLLABORATIVE PROBLEM-SOLVING IN THE ENCHANTED FOREST
AVRIL BROCK

We went into the forest.
River deep and river wide,
Please let me cross to the other side.
Why did we go into the forest?
What did we have to find?
We had to look for Kaliya.
What happened?
We had to solve the clues.

Once upon a time, in a small village in Pakistan there were two children called Nazia and Ilyas, who lived with their parents, grandfather and their pet dog Kaliya. Every night Nana-Ji would tell them stories about an Enchanted Forest near the village. Nazia and Ilyas listened to these stories with interest and amazement. Then they would lie in bed and wonder if all the things that happened in the Forest were really true.

One sunny morning Nazia and Ilyas went to collect some firewood, with Kaliya following behind. After collecting all the wood they could carry, they decided to make their way home. Suddenly Ilyas noticed that Kaliya was not there. Nazia and Ilyas looked everywhere for Kaliya but he was nowhere to be seen.

The only place the children had not looked was in the Enchanted Forest. Ilyas refused to go into the Forest because of what Nana-ji had told them, but Nazia was determined to find Kaliya and would not return home without him.

'You must come with me, Kaliya might be in trouble, and anyway whatever Nana-Ji has told us is just stories, they are not true.'

The children made their way towards the Enchanted Forest. As they came closer they were astonished to hear Kaliya barking in the distance. 'I told you so, Kaliya is in there,' said Nazia. The children reluctantly entered the Forest and as they walked deeper inside, it became darker and strange noises could be heard, noises not normally heard in a forest...

The Forest and the tasks were introduced to the children through this story, and then the children were asked if they would help us look for Kaliya the dog. The young listeners were enraptured by the visitors, fourth year B.Ed. students from Bradford College, telling the story in English and Urdu, and they eagerly agreed to search for the dog. Their class teacher, Maggie Power, was a keen storyteller and the children were used to entering into the spirit and role-playing of stories. She asked the children whether they would be frightened about going into an Enchanted Forest and suggested that they might need protection from spirits or jinns (see Chapter 4 for fuller explanations of the jinns). She had some magic cloaks which they could borrow to wear in the Forest. 'Should we make a note of the names of the first group of children who go and search, in case anything happens to them?' The first group of five children willingly left the classroom with the students and chattered excitedly about doing something out of the ordinary.

The group walked around the school playground and the students asked the children if they knew if there was a forest nearby. Their explorations took them towards the school library and parents' meeting room. The door was locked, but fortunately the students happened to have a bunch of keys. Perhaps one would open the door, maybe magic words would help. The children gave some suggestions and the door did open. They repeated this with an inner door and the children slowly entered the darkened room. It was a sunny day and beams of light sneaked in between gaps in the blacked-out windows, creating an illuminating and eerie effect on the Forest. The children explored the room – crawling through the tunnel, creeping around the suspended trees, following each other into the palace and crouching down into the cave. They were encouraged to use the stepping stones across the river and to chant the phrase

> River deep and river wide,
> Please let me cross to the other side.

The children were given torches to help them explore and examine the environment as they searched for the dog Kaliya. The dramatic tension was heightened when they heard a dog barking in Forest (– a hidden tape recording!). After they had finished searching, the children were hustled out of the room and into the library next door. There they enthusiastically told another student about what had happened. She helped them to explain their adventures in graphic detail.

The other students returned to the classroom and explained to the rest of the class that the first group of children had got lost in a tunnel in the

Forest. Their cloaks had been found on the floor of the Forest. Would another group of children be brave enough to help in the search? More children volunteered and off they went on the same journey of discovery and exploration. Unfortunately, this group also disappeared in the cave. Then a further group of children melted into the mysterious palace and Mrs Ali (a student) was mysteriously 'sucked up' into one of the trees in the Forest!

The remaining children in the classroom were by now becoming a little nervous and apprehensive about going into the Forest. Maggie said they must all go and find out what had happened to the others. There was some clutching of hands by the children on this last expedition and a great commotion when they heard Kaliya barking in the Forest.

Fortunately, no one had nightmares that night, as the class had a drama and storytelling session in the Forest later that day. The children used the opportunity to investigate, touching the trees, putting their hands in the waterfall and tickling the spiders. They explored all of the Forest – crawling under the tunnel, creeping through the palace and crouching down in the cave.

Maggie organised the children into six groups each of five children, mixing them in ability, friendship, gender, language and culture. This gave the children a broad range of strengths and expectations to bring to the practical experiences. Each group visited the Enchanted Forest once a week for six weeks. Most were bilingual, the majority speaking Panjabi/Urdu as their first language.[1]

The research focused on two aspects: how children engaging in problem-solving work together in a collaborative way with little teacher direction and how they negotiate meaning. To facilitate this, clue cards were positioned with blutac around the Forest and new clues were introduced each week. These could be easily removed and carried to wherever the task was to be undertaken and could be read again and again if necessary. Each visit would follow the same format of five clues, which described the tasks to be undertaken. The clues were written in rhyme and followed the storytelling theme. The children had to negotiate the meanings conveyed on the clue cards, interpret the problems and then begin to undertake the tasks.

The first clue informed the children that they had to find a key. Since the key was magic, it could not be held and a vehicle had to made be for its transportation. Next they had to construct a bridge so that the key could be transported over the river to the palace. The children had to use a precise number of materials and follow the instructions carefully. The materials provided included sheets of newspaper, sellotape, technical lego, wheels, tyres, axles, rods and a small box.

TASK 1

CLUE 1

Through the tunnel you must go.
Do not look up; look down below.

CLUE 2

Now that you have solved the first clue.
Read on further to see what you must do.
Look to the left, look to the right.
Can you see an owl in flight?

CLUE 3

Towit towoo, towit towoo, towoo towit.
Now you must discover a gadget.
Look in the water to find and see
A box to open, what can it be?

CLUE 4

Do not be misled by this key.
This may be the answer to set Kaliya free.
Many powers this key has I'm told,
No longer than 5 seconds must you it hold.
If you do not follow this advice,
Kaliya will pay a terrible price.

CLUE 5

Across the river you must go with the key,
To the palace where the key should be.
Think of ways how this can be done,
Use the tools and have some fun.
Remember that you must not carry this key,
Remember the warnings and set Kaliya free.

When the children entered the Enchanted Forest during the second week, the key had mysteriously disappeared. The children eventually found it weighed down in a pool of water in the middle of the river. (Please use your imagination to transform a square trough of water into a naturalistic pool in the river.) The children had to make a boat that would be waterproof, stable and buoyant in order to transport the key across the pool and river. The materials to be used were written as a list in the final clue. A time limit of fifteen minutes was set using a clock timer.

TASK 2

CLUE 1

Go to the palace and look for the key,
Is it where it really should be?
The key has been taken from this place
And put in a completely different place.

CLUE 2

Look up, look down, look all around.
The key is in the water not on the ground.
Wait, be careful, stop and think.
Do not touch the water or the key will sink.

CLUE 3

The key is heavy, it is fastened to a weight.
Get it across before it is too late.
The key has magic powers, do not it hold,
You have fifteen minutes. Now you' ve been told.

CLUE 4

You must build a boat to carry the key.
Use the materials that you see.
Repeat this riddle to solve the problem:
    The boat must be waterproof and not get wet.
    The boat must be stable and not get upset.
    The boat must be buoyant and must not sink yet.

CLUE 5

There is a limit to what you can choose.
Think carefully before you lose.
To keep Kaliya safe and the magic tight.
Follow this list and use the things right.

3 SHEETS OF PAPER; I PIECE OF CARD; 2 POLYTHENE BAGS;
3 STRAWS; 1 PIECE OF STRING; STAPLES; STICKY TAPE.

The following week the task was to make an electric circuit to light a bulb.
Then the children had to make a switch that would allow them to transmit
a signal and so communicate with the jinns. They needed to discover where
the jinns were hiding Kaliya and to ask them to set him free.

Another clue, another puzzle

TASK 3

CLUE 1

Well done! Last week you did really well,
But now there is more story to tell.
The key has gone missing yet again.
Could you search for the clues around this terrain?

CLUE 2

Look around the room, what can you see?
We have some visitors from the Land Of The Tree.
Are they the jinns that Mrs Ali met?
Some of them are too frightening to forget.

CLUE 3

They can see and hear, but they cannot talk,
Do not be afraid they cannot walk.
We need to communicate to find out what they need.
They may have a message that you need to read.

CLUE 4

Which language do you think they will understand?
Will they stay or return to their magic land?
Let us try to signal using a light,
You really need to get this message right.

CLUE 5

Use the materials listed below,
To make a circuit and a light will show.
You need an insulator and a conductor too,
To help the electricity to pass through.
A switch is needed to control the light,
Flash it **ON / OFF / ON / TWICE** to get it right..
That is the message that you need to send
In order to bring this task to the correct end.

1 BATTERY HOLDER; 1 BATTERY; 1 BULB AND BULB HOLDER;
1 YELLOW LEAD; 1 GREEN LEAD; 1 RED LEAD;
1 SILVER PAPER CLIP; 2 GOLDEN PAPER FASTENERS;
SOME SELLOTAPE; SOME SILVER FOIL;
1 SMALL PIECE OF CARD.

Through their oral storytelling, the project team continually reinforced the idea that the jinns had stolen Kaliya. Since this gave the children a definite target, they were highly motivated to complete the tasks successfully. The fourth task was to devise a container to protect the key and to conduct fair tests to find the best materials.

TASK 4

CLUE 1

Now that you are aware of the clues
Surely you will know exactly what to do
Today is a task to protect the key
Using the materials that you can see.

CLUE 2

Remember that you cannot hold the key.
It must be wrapped in the paper that you can see.
Make a decision as to which paper is best;
It's very important that you devise a fair test.

CLUE 3

The paper's protection needs to be waterproof and strong
The parcel that you make must not go wrong.
It must not rip and it must not tear.
Or the magic will escape, SO BEWARE!

CLUE 4

To make a fair test you need to think of what to do;
How much force it takes to pull the paper through.
Think about   1. How much water
                 2. Size of paper
                 3. How to fasten the paper over the beaker
                 4. How many weights
                 5. Anything else that you can think of!

CLUE 5

Don't forget that the test must be fair
So use the materials with extra care.
Remember our aim is to set Kaliya free.
Perhaps by next week a surprise you will see.

The final session in the Enchanted Forest required a definite result and a satisfactory conclusion.

TASK 5

The final clues
You have done well
Your mission is complete.
Now look on the floor
And follow the feet.
Look at the map
And follow the trail.
Look at it carefully,
You have no time to fail.
Don't be alarmed,
Don't be afraid
The key has changed
From its original shape.

Think where to use the key,
Could it be the one to set Kaliya free?

The Chief Jinn appears

The children entered the Forest and followed the clues as they had on the other occasions. This time the clues led them to the palace, where they were surprised to find that there were no tasks, only a map of the Forest.

The children followed arrows and doggy footsteps until they found a box. Inside the box was a large wooden key. They looked around for where the key might fit and discovered a newly built, large wooden door at the entrance of the cave. They inserted the key and the door opened. Kaliya (a black miniature poodle) ran out, to the children's delight and amazement. (It has to be said that Kaliya did not come running quite so quickly for the fourth group of children!) Following Kaliya out of the cave was the chief jinn, Ron – the technician who had helped in the designing and erection of the Enchanted Forest and real owner of Kaliya. The children's reactions exceeded our expectations. They were excited, proud and full of joy that they had succeeded in finding Kaliya.

The children had a wonderful time in the Enchanted Forest, and they enjoyed everything they found there, but they also worked hard at reading the clues, negotiating the meanings and solving the problems. In the imaginative environment the children could easily become actively involved in the story. They quickly learned the procedures and realised that they needed to collaborate to try out the tasks. They realised that they needed to follow the clues without adult guidance. They became self-sufficient – supporting and scaffolding each other's learning and understanding. Quiet children were absorbed in the tasks and in the group work. Many children had the chance to assume leadership and demonstrate personal expertise. Children who were not particularly articulate or confident found that they had valuable knowledge and experience to offer in the scientific activities. All the children demonstrated sustained concentration and involvement and they were eager to participate and get things right.

Research has highlighted the importance of the context in which children learn and the influence it has upon learning. It is evident that children's motivation, curiosity and willingness to learn is stimulated by the learning environment. Donaldson (1978) argues that children understand more successfully when the task is set in a meaningful context. This encourages them to abstract the experience and encode it in language. Carter (1990) suggests that children have a wider range of linguistic resources than we educators give them credit for or realise. Our Enchanted Forest provided the context and opportunity for children to 'use language – to talk and to listen, to argue and agree.'

Vygotsky (1962) observes that adult support is crucial to develop children's thinking. Children also have vast potential for learning through interaction with their environment, accommodating and assimilating their experiences. Piaget (1967 in Wood, 1988) asserts the importance of learning through discovery. Language follows the development of the intellect and an important use of language for children is presenting an argument so that listeners understand the speaker's intentions. The role of the adult is to model, initiate and guide children towards interacting with one another.

The majority of classroom discourse is centred on the teacher. She decides who talks, when and for how long. She asks the questions and anticipates answers which she then evaluates. The most prevalent form of classroom discourse strategy is thus identified as initiation, response, evaluation (Edwards and Westgate, 1994). Children's responses to teachers' questions are often very brief. 'Open' questions with answers that that are not prescriptive and which allow a range of different answers, are less often asked of them.

The work in the Forest was designed to gradually withdraw adult support and let the children explore the language and scientific concepts offered in the problem-solving tasks. Pollard and Tann (1993) advocate strategies for developing collaborative discussion groups, to move children away from teacher dependency. Children may often sit together in groups, but they are rarely trained in the skills for group work (Bennett, 1976; Bennett and Dunne, 1990). Too often child discourse is resource-based and at a low level of social chat, requiring only basic interpersonal communicative skills and not cognitive academic language proficiency (Cummins, 1984). It is therefore important that children are encouraged to participate in group work that enables them to be proactive and collaborative.

Children enter the classroom with a wide range of experiences – what children learn will depend largely on what they already know (Wells, 1987). A collaborative approach that demands that children negotiate encourages children to explore their understanding of a topic (Wells, 1987). In this way, knowledge has to be constructed afresh by each individual knower, through an interaction between the members of the group. The teacher needs to develop strategies that are built into a style of interaction that is supportive and collaborative.

Children use language to maintain relationships, to express themselves individually and most importantly to frame questions. Many pupils feel more confident talking to their peers than when talking to the adult who controls the classroom discourse. Furthermore they are often better able to grasp concepts more effectively when these are transmitted through the understanding and the words of another pupil. For children to develop their understanding they need to be able to challenge, clarify, appraise and defend their knowledge through discussion, explanation and debate. Barnes and Todd (1977) show that handing over the control of talk to pupils would make a wider range of speech acts available to them. So it is important to create situations where such discussion can take place. Children need to feel that they are important individuals with ideas that are valuable.

The research project in the Enchanted Forest facilitated the gathering of a large amount of transcribed child discourse. It is useful to be able to review children's talk in such a form, as it can provide an insight into how children think and learn (Wood, 1988, Fisher, 1990, 1995.) Samples of the discourse transcribed highlight key aspects of children's talk. On reading, transcripts may often appear to be fragmented, full of repetitions, hesitations and irrelevancies, but knowledge of the context and situation helps the researcher in the analysis and evaluation. In the following transcripts the adult's talk is in italics, so that her gradually reducing role and therefore the enhanced collaboration of the children, as they came to understand the expectations of the tasks, can be readily observed.

In this initial introduction the adult inducts the children into the role of the clues and procedures they were expected to follow each time they entered the Enchanted Forest.

> Through the tunnel you must go; Do not look up look down below.
> *What have you got to do then? Let's look at the clue again, what does it tell you to do?*
> There, let me read them all again.
> (Reads the written clues)
> Do not be misled by the key.
> We need some sticks and some paper to make the bridge go across the river.
> We help people to get the key. Think how this can be done.

The children needed to read the clues until they understood them and to keep rereading them to remind themselves of the ultimate objectives.

> **CLUE 1**.........do not look up, look down below.
> Shall we go into the castle?
> **CLUE 2** Now that you have found the first clue. Read on further to see what you must do.

Look to the left, look to the right. Can you see an owl in flight?
What did it tell you to do?
CLUE 3 Towit towoo, towit towoo, towoo towit. Now you must
discover a gadget.
Look in the water to find and see. A box to open, what can it be?
It's a key; another message.
Another message. The key's here.
CLUE 4 Do not be misled by this key. This may be the answer to set
Kaliya free. Many powers this key has I'm told. No longer than five
seconds must you it hold.
If you do not follow this advice, Kaliya will pay a terrible price.
CLUE 5 Across the river you must go with the key, To the palace is
where the key should be.
Think of ways this can be done. Use the tools and have some fun.
Remember that you must not carry this key. Remember the warnings
and set Kaliya free.
Don't pick that key up.
No, put it down; put it in the box.
It's in the box, so you're O.K. What did it say not to do?

The children immediately related to the clues, adapted to the story's theme
and followed the instructions. They accepted the magic without thinking,
automatically suspending their disbelief. This is apparent throughout all the
sessions.

It's magic though. We need help, how will we get that over the river?
This key's got more powers.
What if somebody comes?
Is this a magic stick?

The adult role initially is to direct the children and enable them to become
autonomous in their learning. She can then withdraw almost completely, to
observe the children negotiating the meanings and the problems themselves. She will support, prompt, ask questions and gently reinforce when
necessary, but will keep passing the initiative back to the children so they
learn to work things out for themselves.

You can't pick this key up.
How long can you hold it for?
Five seconds.
It says five seconds here.
You must hold it for no longer than five seconds.

With some teacher encouragement the children are learning to reread the clues until they are clear about the intentions. They occasionally became distracted and start to search fervently around the Forest for the lost dog. The adult has to gently refocus them. Her role is to direct the children in the procedures and to question them.

So where's the dog, where are the clues?
... this dog, we can't find it anywhere.
So what are you going to have to do?
Doggy, come here, come on.
Carry on and look.
Maybe you should read those clues again if they are the only clues.
... you must go with the clues.
Read it further.
You must go the palace where the key should be
Right, but you can't hold it so how are you going to put it down in five seconds?
So how are you going to cross the river, what did it say?
Across the river with the key.
It doesn't tell us.
So how are you going to do it?
We still can't find the dog.
Because you are not doing what you are supposed to be doing, you have to think about it. Read the clues, you have to read the clues again to do exactly what it tells you.
Have you got the clues? What did they tell you to do? Read them carefully.
You've got to get it across the river.
Yes, you've got to get it across the river.
It says something about the tools.
Yes, It does say something about the tools.
How are you going to stick it on?
Do you have to make four wheels?
What do you think?
How are we going to put the key?
Look you put the key on there, the back.
Right, how are you going to put them on the car?
Look, you've got to put the wheels on there like this.

Gradually it becomes less and less necessary for the teacher to prompt directly. The children begin to grasp what is expected and are prompted by the written clues themselves and the resources provided. They become focused upon the problems and learn how to follow the expected procedures.

Everybody listen to Sajid.
You can't make a bridge. You've got to make a boat out of all of this.
I've got it, I've got it. We've got to make a boat.
You read it again then.
Across the river you must go, the key ... put it down
We need more sticks and more newspaper.
Miss, we need to tie it.

The children are now actively involved in the task of making a bridge. They are questioning and thinking for themselves. They are solving the problem together, asking each other questions. They have learnt to read the clues in order, and they read them all before they start to work on the task in hand. They take turns to read a clue. They can now direct themselves and are using the clues successfully to introduce the task to be undertaken and then to check if they have done it correctly. However, they still ask for reassurance from the adult to see if they had got it right.

I know what you have to do then.
What do you have to do?
What do you have to make?
You have to make a circuit.
Read this and we make a circuit.
Possibly not, yes we've made a circuit already.
Put it back here, move it.
Battery then, we need another box.
We need a battery as well.
She's got a battery.
We've got to put it here.
We need another one.
Don't make a fuss.
How like ..., we need the stuff out of here.
A battery, battery, battery.
You're making a fuss.
Give me a battery, I know what to do.
This is ..., what's that?
You have to stick that in there.
And this, like this.
The battery might not work.
Push this on or 3 or 4 on.
No, let him do it.
Let me hold the battery down and then I've done it.
Make a circuit.
Pick that up there, pick it up and put it here.

This way, you need this.
Miss, we've done it, Miss, we've made it, yes Miss, we've made it.
Read the list, one battery, one battery holder, yellow card, one yellow
lead, one green lead, one red lead.
Miss, we've just made it.

Because the children's language is contextually embedded in their actions,
it may be difficult to determine exactly what is going on. However, there is
immediate feedback in their conversations which minimises vagueness and
ambiguity.

We need one more wire.
Got one, got one. You put the wire here.
No, no pass it there.
You put the wire on there.
The wire's broken.
We need another one.
A nice one.
We'll put this switch on, give me that.
No, I have to put that.
The light won't come on.
Check all the wire's up.
Why?
It won't work, look.
I think this is the ba ...
No, I have to turn it the other way, I think.
No, you don't have to.
Yes, it's that way, that way.

You can almost hear the brain cells clicking away as the children think
through the problem in hand. Their busy hands are manipulating the wires
to make the connections and the switch. You can almost hear the logical
reasoning taking place as the children question each other and build their
own understanding based on each others' ideas.

Yes, there, Miss we've done it.
How can you switch it on and off? To send the message?
Miss, one off, one on, one off, one on.
(Several children speaking together)
If you turn one off they them both will ...
Put it like that.
Look if I take mine off, they both will come off.

A timely question by the adult interrupts and redirects the children, reminding them that the aim of the task is to communicate with the jinns through a coded message by switching the light off and on. The children attack the task with renewed vigour and again begin to question and reason. Can you make something so that you don't have to keep taking it off and putting it back on, can you make a switch? The adult had decided to get involved, because she felt that the children thought they had completed the task correctly. In order to keep them working and prevent them from waiting for further instructions she decided to challenge the children and push them towards a further goal.

Once they had established what they had to do, the children were able to organise themselves and allot roles in order to solve the problem. The children worked together and discussed the tasks in a collaborative manner. Gender differences were occasionally noted within the groups – at times boys and girls would work collaboratively, but occasionally they would split into small groups of all girls or all boys. Occasionally a dominant child would control the discourse, giving instructions and taking the lead. But many incidences such as 'a circuit we need to make' demonstrated an appreciation of the need for the whole group to work together. They were able to be proactive in managing their own learning in the imaginative context and they collaborated in the tasks. Some who were less articulate found that they had knowledge and experience that was useful for solving in the scientific problems.

The children needed situations in which they could reflect upon their learning and engagement in the problems set. This was achieved through reporting and describing the events to an audience. At the end of each visit to the Forest they reported to a member of the research team who had not witnessed their efforts. They were eager to talk about their experiences. They explained the activities, defining the meanings of the clues and the vocabulary used. Probing questions elicited explanations that showed that the children could describe the problems and define the vocabulary. They could use the targeted vocabulary in the context of the activities and demonstrated that they knew the meaning of the words.

The research team returned to the school four months after the project had finished to talk to the children and see what they remembered and whether they could reflect upon their work. Lisa, Sarah and Carol asked the children to answer the following questions that targeted the scientific concepts, the process skills used and the language embedded in the tasks:

Bridge and buggy

What is a bridge?
How did you make the bridge?
Why did you make it that way? e.g. more stronger, stable.
Was paper a good material to use?
What are bridges normally made of?
Was the buggy easy to make?

Floating and sinking

Can you remember making a 'boat' for the key?
How did you make it?
What were the important factors for making the boat?
Did shape, size, weight affect its ability to float?
What did the boat have to be so as not to sink?
Why was this important?

Electric circuit

How did you make the electric circuit?
Why do you think it is called a 'circuit'?
Why did the light bulb light up?
What does conductor mean?
Will electricity flow through any material?
Which materials won't it flow through?
What is a switch?
How does this work?

Fair test

What does 'fair test' mean?
How did you devise a fair test?
How did you decide which material to use?
Why is a fair test important?

The children demonstrated that they could reflect upon the work they did in the Forest and gave appropriate and accurate responses to the questions. They struggled with the questions about the fair testing and needed some guidance from the adults. The children could use the targeted vocabulary that communicated some of more complex meanings. The story framework and the Forest environment had helped the children's concept development, supported memory and recall, and had provided an excellent vehicle for learning.

All the children said that they had learnt a lot and that they had enjoyed collaborating and helping each other. They had enjoyed solving problems, working through the clues, finding out how to do things and make things. They enjoyed working in the Forest and they wanted to do it all again. Although they had learned so much, it had not felt to them like a proper lesson.

Note
1. Many of the children spoke Panjabi as their first language, but they were all fluent in the status language of Urdu. We have decided to use the phrase 'first language' throughout this book as this is the most accurate label we can achieve. But several of the children probably learned two first languages simultaneously from parents and grandparents. 'First language' is nonetheless the best term, giving a clearer message than 'home', 'heritage', 'community' or 'mother tongue,' as the children's language use was not restricted in these ways. We refer to their language as Panjabi/Urdu, because most of the children code-switched between these two languages, using aspects of sentence structure and vocabulary from both.

CHAPTER 2
DEVELOPING SCIENCE IN THE ENCHANTED FOREST

JOHN HOLLINGWORTH AND AVRIL BROCK

Solving problems can be a motivating link between science and technology (Johnston, 1996) and a good problem-solving activity will start from the children's own interests. The teacher's task in initiating a problem to be solved is to make it broad enough and interesting enough to involve and guide the children's participation in the learning processes. It is not just by doing, but by thinking, that children learn new procedures and concepts, so it is vital to allow children to express their thinking in scientific and technological contexts. This can be achieved by letting the children explore, investigate, discover and research using a broad range of resources and activities.

Children need practical experiences which allow them to make the connections between procedural and conceptual understanding. According to Johnston (1996) the main aim of teachers of science should be to develop positive scientific attitudes in children along with knowledge, skill and concepts. This was promoted in the Enchanted Forest through the imaginative setting and the story context.

This book centres on the importance of children communicating, exploring and expressing their ideas through interactive discussion. They need to put their thoughts into words that others will understand and be able to clarify and refine their ideas (Barnes, 1976). It is crucial that children realise that they do not have to get everything 'right' first time, that their explorations can be tentative and will be subject to modification as they build upon each others' ideas. They need to become open minded. Pupils need opportunities to explore, activities that encourage curiosity and problems that allow them to be creative and inventive (Johnston, 1996).

Harlen (in Johnston, 1996) identifies four possible causes of lack of curiosity in children: temperament, experience, environment and social constraints. For children to be enthusiastic about science they need a range of experiences and activities that can be accessed in different ways. Only then will the learning needs of girls and boys of different ages and cultures be met. The environment of the Enchanted Forest allowed children to explore aspects of the curriculum in different ways. Their explorations and problem-solving experiences, contextual relevance and the shared experiences in 'real' time provoked the motivation on which to build a structured engagement with science.

Children today demand stimulating activities that will motivate their learning. By giving them activities of this nature, teachers can 'develop a creative teaching approach which challenges stereotypical views of science and, most clearly, develops knowledge alongside skills' (Johnston, 1996). Johnston acknowledges that it is hard for teachers to provide original, stimulating ideas which enthuse children. Not all children are necessarily curious about science and they must be motivated to want to learn more. In Chapter 9, Maggie Power emphasises the power of the Enchanted Forest for motivating work both inside the Forest and back in the classroom.

As teachers we need to know our subject, be enthusiastic about it, understand how children learn and have a repertoire of interesting ideas. Positive attitudes towards science need to be developed at primary level if children are to succeed with scientific study in secondary education. Attitudes influence learning and affect how we react to people, objects and events. Encouragement and example help to develop positive attitudes to science for children that 'cannot be taught in the way specific facts and skills can be; they are often transferred in subtle and often unsuspected ways' (Harlen, 1993).

The Association for Science Education (Sherrington, 1993) argues that a relevant contextual framework is an important aspect of effective science teaching. This can be achieved by creating a complete environment to work in that makes children look and think from fresh perspectives. Making learning activities meaningful to children, gives purpose to problem-solving. The quest for Kaliya, the discovery of the key and the challenge of rescuing the dog from the jinns motivated the children to explore and investigate through story and role-play.

Children need to achieve personal success and understanding through pupil-generated activity as well as through teacher dependence, and tasks were planned and organised accordingly. Thorough planning was important to enable the children to follow their own investigative pathways. If we give children ownership of the learning and a purpose for their activity their involvement and understanding will be far greater.

The clues were patterned to be read and thought through. That directed the children to carry out their problem-solving and scientific exploration in a progressive manner. Children need to have numerous experiences that connect events in a sequence so that they can understand the notion of cause being related to effect. Action and thinking are closely related and children need to carry out actions and practise skills in meaningful contexts to promote conceptual development. Harlen (1993) demonstrates how children 7 to 9 years old are gradually developing the power to use of thought instead of action, seeing a simple process as a whole, seeing events as part of a sequence. They begin to think things through in reverse, realise that two effects need to be taken into account, envisage things from another's point of view and relate a physical cause to its effect.

Young children are concerned with the familiar and they are dependent on visual impression. Quantities that can be manipulated in the mind are those that are seen and easily represented. The complexity of the problem influences the children's ability and approach. Many children do not see the point of what they do and are far from making a connection with the world around them (Osborne and Freyberg, 1985). Children need to see the relevance of what they are doing – the story set in the Forest provided real problems for the children to solve.

As knowledge and skills develop, the content should be increased beyond the immediately familiar so that there is development in the way children find out about things. The Enchanted Forest provided such an environment, extending children's existing experience and inducing them to work collaboratively. They were set problem-solving tasks in which they needed to draw on their own and each other's resources and experiences. The adults provided the problems but not the instructions for solving them.

When undertaking scientific activities in class, children are often directed into small groups to encourage the sharing of ideas. For this to be effective the children have to be cooperative, tolerant, flexible and sensitive. The environment of the Forest and the tasks required to find Kaliya facilitated the children's cooperation. They worked together, often in an excited way, sometimes solving an aspect of the task individually, but usually bringing results together in order to get a corporate conclusion. This required little teacher direction. Children achieved personal responsibility in working towards the end result. They made decisions and resolved difficulties.

Barnes (1976) stresses the importance of children communicating with each other in their learning. Children need to think openly and out loud, because talking is essential to learning. 'The teacher's absence removes from their work the usual source of authority; they cannot turn to her to solve dilemmas. Thus children not only formulate hypotheses but are compelled to evaluate them for themselves.' The session at the end of each visit when the children reported back to a 'new' adult, proved to be invaluable. Further opportunities for review and discussion were given at intervals of three months and one year. Maggie Power illustrates the long term memories of the children in Chapter 9.

Children need to be introduced to scientific vocabulary on a continual basis. For example, when learning an additional language we often need to hear a word as much as sixteen times before it becomes part of our active vocabulary. Learning science terminology is perhaps not dissimilar. Many of the words used in science are not only new items of terminology but they often also carry new concepts and ideas that have to be accommodated and assimilated into children's understanding. Children need to hear these words in situations where they are related to an activity and have a meaning that can gradually be perceived and understood. 'It does children no service to provide words which they cannot use to convey meaning because they do not realise what meaning the word has' observes Harlen (1993). She stresses that children need to be aware that some words may have a more precise meaning in scientific terms than when used in everyday life. Non-scientific words used in a science context may take on different meanings and children need to to gain an understanding of how words work in different situations. Chapter 3 shows the children's responses and their understanding of the meaning of selected vocabulary read in the clues. We now evaluate children's responses to the problems they tackled.

Problem 1 – Over the Bridge

To solve the first problem, the children were required to construct a bridge over a river. It had to be strong enough to support a vehicle carrying the key, but the only construction materials were newspaper and sticky tape, which meant that they had to find ways of making strong structures from flimsy resources. A construction kit was provided for making the vehicle. They needed to design a chassis appropriate for attaching axles and wheels. This would in turn lead to them creating a rolling 'buggy' that could be pulled across the bridge with a length of string.

The children began the bridge building task with great enthusiasm and there was no shortage of ideas in this initial stage. While bombarding each

Science learning objectives:

Objective		NC references KS 1	KS2
1.	To investigate the strength of different shapes and structures	Sc3 2a	
2.	To investigate ways of using paper to create strong structures	Sc3 1e, 2a	Sc3 1a
3.	To explore and describe ways of making things move	Sc4 2a	
4.	To explore how forces make things move	Sc4 2c	
5.	To ask questions and use focused exploration and investigation to acquire scientific knowledge, understanding and skills	Sc0 1a, 1b	Sc0 1a, 1b
6.	To use first hand experience to obtain information	Sc0 1c	Sc0 1c
7.	To turn ideas into a form that can be investigated	Sc1 1a	Sc1 1a
8.	To understand the usefulness of making predictions when planning what to do	Sc1 1b	Sc1 1b
9.	To explore and make observations using appropriate senses	Sc1 2a, 2b	Sc1 2b
10.	To communicate what happens during their work	Sc1 3a	
11.	To make comparisons	Sc1 3	

other with comments such as 'we need to put sticks underneath it' and 'we should put paper across here', they excitedly explored the materials. Although little actual construction work took place at this point, it was clearly an important stage. A great deal of thinking was going on as the children considered ideas, drawing upon their prior experiences. Gradually ideas began to turn into actions and the children started to fasten the materials together. This early work was not particularly systematic and children often worked individually or in pairs rather than as a whole group, but their enthusiasm for the environment and story theme was clear for all to see.

A critical point in the task came when a someone suggested that they needed to make the paper stronger. A number of ideas were offered, such as 'we could make something like a table' and 'we could make a box.' One child's response was to roll up a piece of paper into a tube. With timely intervention, the teacher drew attention to this and showed the group how to make tight, strong tubes by rolling the paper around a piece of dowelling. Suddenly, the early exploratory work became more purposeful, with all the children working together to create a stockpile of tubes. In response to another child's suggestion, the tubes were fastened together with sticky tape, put in place across the river and then covered in paper to complete the bridge. This was an intense and purposeful period of work, with excellent concentration and cooperation to finish the task.

While the majority of children were working on the bridge, one boy was intently engaged on constructing the buggy. He was single-minded in his actions and did not particularly respond to the occasional suggestions of others. It was evident that he was familiar with the construction kit and confident about using it. The rest of the team soon began to check on his progress and achievements and the team spirit was maintained. When the construction work finished, the group enthusiastically completed the task by transporting the key across the bridge. They became involved with the story again, and were very excited about what was to happen next!

With regard to the intended learning objectives, a great deal of purposeful cooperative work was undoubtedly taking place. The children were enthusiastically exploring, investigating and communicating ideas to each other. There was much questioning and predicting as the group grappled with the problem, mostly generated by the children in response to the task rather than being structured by the teacher.

As mentioned, the early work was not very systematic and a case could be made for prior work on structures in the classroom to provide a basis of knowledge upon which the children could have drawn when faced with the same problems in the context of the Forest. Nevertheless, it was encouraging to see how many children could confidently offer ideas for solving the task. All the group were engaged in bridge building, and thus able to develop their understanding about the construction and strength of structures.

Only one or two children were involved in constructing the buggy so the potential of this activity for the exploration of scientific knowledge about forces and motion was confined purely to the problem to be solved. In order to focus properly on this area of science, constructing the buggy might be best undertaken as a separate activity. Pairs or small groups could perhaps each have made a buggy and then compared and discussed designs, either as a preparatory exercise or follow up activity using the same basic problem as a starting point.

Problem 2 – Crossing the water

For the second problem, the children were required to construct a boat which would carry the key across a stretch of water. Paper, card, art straws and polythene bags were provided as construction materials, and the children had to design and make a craft which was waterproof, stable and buoyant enough to float across a pool with the key aboard.

Science learning objectives:

Objective		NC references KS 1	KS2
1.	To investigate the use of materials for constructing a boat and relate the use of these materials to their properties	Sc3 1a, 1e	Sc3 1a
2.	To gain awareness of the factors involved in flotation, and the forces acting on floating objects	Sc4 2f, 2g, 2h	
3.	To ask questions and use focused exploration and investigation to acquire scientific knowledge, understanding and skills	Sc0 1a, 1b	Sc0 1a, 1b
4.	To use first hand experience to obtain information	Sc0 1c	Sc0 1c
5.	To relate scientific ideas to the evidence for them	Sc0 3a	Sc0 3b
6.	To understand and use scientific vocabulary, including stability, waterproof, buoyancy	Sc0 4a	Sc0 4a
7.	To turn ideas into a form that can be investigated	Sc1 1a	Sc1 1a
8.	To understand the usefulness of making predictions when planning what to do	Sc1 1b	Sc1 1b
9.	To explore and make observations using appropriate senses	Sc1 2a, 2b	Sc1 2b
10.	To communicate what happens during their work	Sc1 3a	

The problem was presented to the children as a written clue which indicated that a successful boat would need to be 'waterproof, stable and buoyant'. There was some initial discussion with the teacher about the meaning of these words. Most of the children were familiar with the word 'waterproof', and understood it to mean that 'water can't get in'. A few children however, attached the reverse meaning to the word, and suggested that it meant 'water goes on something and it will sink'. The word 'stable' was familiar for its alternative meaning, with one child suggesting it was 'a place for horses,' but the idea of stability with respect to steadiness and balance was not really understood at this stage. 'Buoyancy' was also an unfamiliar word to most of them, but because of the context of the boat

On task

building task, the children recognised that all these words had something to do with preventing a boat sinking.

When presented with the construction materials, the children were at first very uncertain about what to do. Their first course of action was to explore the materials in rather a random fashion, touching, feeling and bending the items whilst considering how to proceed. This exploratory stage, though seeming rather purposeless, is clearly important, and the physical manipulation was undoubtedly helping the children to think about how to tackle the problem. However, it did require some prompts from the teacher to move them forward from this stage. She suggested that they begin by making the shape of the boat using cardboard and asked them how the structure could be made waterproof, while drawing their attention to the polythene bags.

Once a start had been made on the construction, the children grew in confidence and new ideas developed out of their actions and deliberations. Most of the resulting structures were flat rafts covered in polythene. None of the groups made a container shape or thought to inflate the polythene bags to create more buoyancy. Some of the details of their designs were clearly determined by ideas of what a boat should look like rather than suitability for the immediate problem. For example, some groups used straws to make masts which in actual fact were of no use in helping the structure to float. This clearly demonstrates the children's need to work in a concrete rather than an abstract manner at this stage. When tested, all the boats completed the task of carrying the key across a stretch of water, thus ensuring a successful and satisfactory conclusion.

The children gained invaluable experience of undertaking an open-ended task. They were able to turn ideas into actions, and the task provided rich opportunities for questioning, first hand exploration and communication with each other. They effectively learned about the use of materials for constructing boats. Although their understanding of the specific terms (waterproof, stable and buoyant) was less certain at this stage, later discussion with the children (referred to in Chapters 3 and 7) showed that many of them could discuss the word meanings related to the context and to previous experience. Children do not necessarily use specific scientific vocabulary while undertaking a practical task. They may not have met this subject-based language previously and are able to construct successfully without using the technical language. It is after they have completed the task that the children can be helped to verbalise what they had demonstrated practically.

The children need to be able to explore problems, to think things through and to try to accommodate new learning and practical application through experiential situations. The spontaneity, the stimulating environment of the Forest and the context of the problem all helped to create an atmosphere of excitement and enthusiasm which had a powerful influence upon the children's motivation and concentration.

Problem 3 – Sending a signal

For the third problem, the children were required to transmit a signal to communicate with the jinns. This involved assembling an electrical circuit to light a bulb, and then constructing a switch from simple materials (card, paper clips, paper fasteners, tinfoil and sellotape) so that the bulb could be turned on and off to send a signal.

Science learning objectives:

Objective		NC references KS 1	KS2
1.	To construct a simple circuit using batteries, wires and bulbs	Sc4 1b	
2.	To know that a complete circuit is needed for electrical devices to work, and understand how a switch can be used to control devices in a circuit	Sc4 1a, 1b	
3.	To understand how a switch works, and design a switch using simple materials	Sc3 1e	Sc3 1a, 1c
4.	To ask questions and use focused exploration and investigation to acquire scientific knowledge, understanding and skills	Sc0 1a, 1b	Sc0 1a, 1b
5.	To use first hand experience to obtain information	Sc0 1c	Sc0 1c
6.	To understand and use scientific vocabulary, including circuit switch, conductor, insulator	Sc0 4a	Sc0 4a
7.	To turn ideas into a form that can be investigated	Sc1 1a	Sc1 1a
8.	To understand the usefulness of making predictions when planning what to do	Sc1 1b	Sc1 1b
9.	To consider what apparatus and equipment to use	Sc1 1e	
10.	To explore and make observations using appropriate senses	Sc1 2a, 2b	Sc1 2b
11.	To communicate what happens during their work	Sc1 3a	

The first part of the task was to construct an electrical circuit from a battery, a bulb and wires. One child from the group immediately and confidently began assembling the components while the others looked on. Through his previous experience of these resources he was able to model an approach to the problem that the rest of the group quickly emulated. Gradually they all joined in, at first by offering advice such as 'this goes there, look' and 'join the clip to that place' and then by taking a more active role.

As their confidence increased, there was some argument about the correct method, and competition to be the one to put the circuit together. Generally however, the group cooperated well. The children clearly had some knowledge of assembling these components and most of the groups soon created a circuit. One group explored the problem of how to achieve it and, with a little prompting from Nazia, slipped into avidly discussing the problem in excited and rapid Panjabi. It was fascinating to observe them, as it was obvious to any onlooker, whether or not they could understand the language, that they were absolutely on task, building on one another's ideas to achieve their objective.

Although the children were familiar with the word 'switch', they did not have a real understanding of how one works, so constructing a switch was beyond them. Very few of the groups constructed the switch using the materials as expected. However they were remarkably inventive, using scissors to create connections or manipulating the resources manually to switch the circuit off and on. Only one group initially failed to complete the circuit correctly. As time went on and the bulb refused to light, this group became frustrated and began to lose interest. They were not systematic in their search for a solution and began joining pieces of card and foil haphazardly to the components. Eventually they looked to Nazia to help them out, and she took them systematically through the construction of a circuit until the bulb was successfully lit. The adult provided some clues, but to achieve their goal successfully, this group of children needed instructions to follow, examples to see, or more prior knowledge.

It was clear from their work that the children's understanding of a circuit developed. They began to understand and use the terms 'conductor', 'insulator' and 'switch.' Although they had initially been unable to define these words, they had clear knowledge of the electrical conductivity of different materials, which Nazia was able to link to the correct scientific terms.

The children's own free explorations were significant. The open-ended switch-making task required them to plan what to do, consider what resources to use and communicate their ideas to the group. These are important skills to develop but, equally, there needs to be enough structure and support for the children to make good progress.

Teacher prompts were provided at appropriate moments to ensure that things were learnt correctly. A critical factor in the success of such open-ended work is to ensure that support and structure is provided before the children become frustrated and lose interest. The children had never met the problem of creating a switch before and it was an interesting and motivating introduction for learning about the need for switches. Once they had perceived the necessity to investigate further, this could be explored back in the classroom situation.

Problem 4 – Protecting the key

For the final problem, the children were required to select an appropriate type of paper in which to wrap the key to protect it and keep it safe. The paper needed to be strong and waterproof, and the task involved devising and carrying out fair tests to identify the best paper for this purpose.

The children began, as with all the tasks, by investigating the materials. By touching, feeling, bending and stretching the different types of paper, they were able to make comparisons and gain information about their physical properties. They moved on to make predictions about the strength and waterproof qualities of each type of paper. However they needed adult guidance to work through testing them systematically. Without this intervention, it is likely that the children would have concentrated their attentions on the paper they thought would be the best, without giving equal consideration to the others. They drew their own conclusions from their previous experiences and paid attention to the visual qualities of the materials. The main objective in the children's minds was to solve the problem. They knew they had to free Kaliya as quickly as possible and hurried to reach their goal.

They tackled the testing of the papers enthusiastically, engaging purposefully in the task, grappling with the demands of generating ideas and turning them into a form which could be investigated. These are difficult skills to master, and the powerful context of the Forest and the story were definitely motivating factors.

Science learning objectives:

Objective		NC references KS 1	KS2
1.	To determine and compare the strength and water resistance of different types of paper, and use this information to select the most appropriate paper for a specific task	Sc3 1a, 1e	Sc3 1a
2.	To ask questions and use focused exploration and investigation to acquire scientific knowledge, understanding and skills	Sc0 1a, 1b	Sc0 1a, 1b
3.	To use first hand experience to obtain information	Sc0 1c	Sc0 1c
4.	To turn ideas into a form that can be investigated	Sc1 1a	Sc1 1a
5.	To understand the usefulness of making predictions when planning what to do	Sc1 1b	Sc1 1
6.	To devise and carry out a fair test	Sc1 1c	Sc1 1c, 1d, 1e
7.	To make careful observations and measurements	Sc1 2b, 2c	Sc1 2b
8.	To communicate what happens during their work	Sc1 3a	
9.	To make comparisons and identify trends in their results	Sc1 3c	Sc1 3b
10.	To draw conclusions and relate them to their predictions	Sc1 3d, 3e	Sc1 3c, 3d

It was interesting to see that the children's ideas were confined to emulating exactly how the paper would be used in the story context. For example, to test for waterproofing, they wrapped the key up in each type of paper and put the parcel into a bowl of water. None of them considered an alternative test which didn't involve wrapping the key. They were solely concerned with solving the specific problem of protecting and transporting the key. This indicates how significant the context of the task is in determining a course of action. The science was matched to the context and the story line constructed around the tasks. These had been organised in such a way as to promote conceptual and procedural development of science in the National Curriculum.

Children need to experience skills and processes if they are to develop an understanding of scientific procedure. When children are faced with something new, they search around in their minds, often subconsciously, and use previous experience to try to understand, linking new ideas to existing ones. Children need to accommodate new ideas and change their existing thinking, by bringing prior knowledge to the fore, relating to new experience and so changing their understanding.

The principle of good science education is that these processes and concepts are not independently developed but are interrelated. That is why the environment of the Enchanted Forest was such a good context. If you just wanted the children to make an electric circuit, they could quite easily copy from the teacher's drawing on a blackboard or worksheet. However if you want the children to apply the process to the concept, it is far better to put them in a situation where they have to investigate and explore at first hand. This way they are more likely to really get to grips with the knowledge. The storyline, the environment of the Forest and the problem-solving activities provided purposeful and exciting situations which effectively involved the children.

The responsive attitude of the teacher to the children's learning is fundamental to creating active learners. 'Children who work only to the teacher's framework for understanding are likely to remain passive learners and be dependent on their ability to think like the teacher' (Ollerenshaw and Ritchie, 1997). Children must have time to orientate their own learning and be challenged to think things through. They need to construct their own approach to learning through a variety of pathways. 'The more a learner is able to control her own language strategies and think aloud, the more she is able to formulate hypotheses and evaluate them' (Ollerenshaw and Ritchie, 1997).

The Enchanted Forest engaged children in contextualised scientific problem-solving. It provided powerful motivation and a memorable shared experience on which to build more structured science work. The activities were designed to elicit the enthusiastic involvement of the children in scientific work which, we hoped, would prompt the use of scientific concepts and terminology. This it did but, as might be expected, the children used the concepts and language in relation to the immediate context and task. They did not generalise scientific models and processes from the task or use more generalised models and procedures in their problem-solving. This project indicates three possible strategies.

1   Experiences of this kind could be used to established the need and relevance of scientific work in the minds of pupils in a motivating and powerfully engaging way, as a basis for more structured follow-up. The value of the experience as a shared and collaborative context would be important here, as would the recontextualisation and decontextualisation of the learning involved.

2   Following more structured preparatory work, experiences of this kind would provide a context in which children would be able to apply procedures, models and principles. Activities could be designed with prompts which referred back to the preparatory work.

3   The activities themselves could be designed in a more structured, staged fashion which would lead the children to explore in a more patterned way.

Whatever the design of the experience and its relationship to preparatory and follow-up work, the enthusiasm and collaborative effort generated by the Enchanted Forest experience, the persistence of the experience in the children's memories and the high level of social and cognitive engagement of all the children, are powerful indicators of the value of this kind of approach in enhancing learning in science.

CHAPTER 3
CHILDREN MAKING MEANING
AND NEGOTIATING
UNDERSTANDING

REBECCA ADAMS, SARA ALI, LAKHBIR KAUR BASSI, NAZIA HUSSAIN AND AVRIL BROCK

As teachers, we face particular linguistic and communicative demands as we promote children's understanding of new concepts within the framework of the National Curriculum. We need to be aware of the language we use to teach and also of the children's use of language and most importantly the links between the two. Once we have established the language common to both parties, we can provide opportunities for children to extend their linguistic experiences and target vocabulary, fundamental to the subjects of the National Curriculum.

We tend to ascribe our expectations of children's understanding according to assumptions we make about their experiences – and these assumptions may well be incorrect. Acknowledging the cultural backgrounds and the implications of the children's personal range of references will help us recognise their connotations and interpretations.

It is not easy to define what we mean by connotation. It involves the context of the situation as well as the intentions of the speaker and the listener – both bring their own experience to the discussion. Until recently classroom research has tended to concentrate on the language strategies used by the teacher, but the language and interpretations of both parties – the teacher and the child – are equally important. This was to be the focus of our research.

A teacher makes specific decisions as to why she is using a particular item of vocabulary, based on her perceptions of what the children know and can do. There is a statement of intention by the teacher as she manages meaning. She uses discourse strategies and selects specific words and phrases. There is interaction between the language used and the context in which it is used. There will be a common connotative link between the words because the teacher will have explicitly set out to achieve this.

The question arises as to whether the teacher's assumptions about the connotations are realistic. Do all the children achieve the intended understanding? There has to be some shared understanding to arrive at an interpretation of the meaning intended. The teacher needs to negotiate the meanings with the children. Listeners do their utmost to make sense of the language they hear, bringing it to bear on it all possible knowledge and interpretation. Learners have a powerful urge to make sense of what is presented to them.

Words are more than their dictionary definitions, they have associations and particular meanings gained through personal and cultural experiences. Adults often use technical explanations when they try to clarify things for a child, but these can leave young children confused and even intellectually defeated. The introduction of a ten subject National Curriculum compounded this problem. The increased need for specialist teaching and for a greater use of subject-specific terminology placed a greater demand on vocabulary expectations within each subject area.

The nature of subject-specific language can confuse and mislead children. Grugeon et al (1998) have researched into teaching and learning subject-specific language within literacy and oracy. They found that younger children use everyday language and experience to describe phenomena that they do not understand. While this may be acceptable during the introduction of new vocabulary and concepts, children need to develop appropriate terminology and understanding that is particular to that subject. McWilliam (1998) demonstrates that 'children's success in curriculum learning depends upon active involvement in building a complex network of linguistic meaning'.

The primary aim of our research was to determine children's understanding of the vocabulary specifically targeted in the Enchanted Forest. We wanted to interpret the connotations and associations the children brought to the learning situations. Ultimately, it is hoped that this research can be used to encourage the enhancement of access to meaning in the curriculum, particularly among children in inner city schools.

Children learn language best in an environment rich with opportunities to explore interesting objects and ideas (Goodman, 1991). 'To get the meaning of anything you do not listen only to the individual words, you comprehend them by awareness of the setting or context in which they occur, and that includes the sentence, the topic, the place, who is speaking, and even the intonation which the speaker uses' (Sutton, 1992). The importance of the social context to the learning and use of language is strongly emphasised in a model which Edwards and Mercer (1987), called the 'cultural communicative' approach.

Children cannot make sense of words in isolation. Rather they need to interact with other people and make connections to their previous experiences to gain understanding. Joan Solomon argues that: 'Pupils in classrooms certainly do not make sense of things just by individual contemplation. Like any other human beings they try out their viewpoints and modes of talking with constant reference to other people who are emotionally significant to them' (in Sutton, 1992). Through doing the tasks in the Forest the children constructed their understanding with each other. Our main concern was to see how the children constructed word meanings and whether this was achieved through the collaborative work. Could the children adapt language used in other situations to meet the demands of the new setting?

The clues which the children had to understand so that they could do the tasks replaced the usual verbal instructions given by a teacher. There were few difficulties in the actual reading of the clues. The urge to get on with the task meant that the children read the clues quickly. They felt a sense of achievement in finding the clues and being able to read them aloud to their group. The rhymes in the clues provided stimulus and motivation and the children began to make up their own rhymes during their experiences in the Forest.

The children's language was sometimes repetitive as they discussed the meanings of the clues because they used repetition in a variety of ways to stress their meaning. They repeated words and phrases, both their own and others', for example: 'bulb and bulb holder'; 'bulb and bulb holder' followed by the paraphrase 'the thingy that holds the bulb'; 'Don't touch the water, don't touch the water, the key will sink'; 'It's in the water, it's in the water'; 'Make a boat, make a boat'.

It is often thought that repetition serves no real purpose but it is really an important factor in increasing and establishing meaning and understanding. 'Repetition is a resource by which conversationalists together create a discourse, a relationship, and a world. It is the central linguistic meaning making strategy' (Tannen, 1989 cited in McCarthy, 1994). The children repeated phrases so that they could be heard by the other children, to make something happen or just through excitement at their accomplishment. They would chat among themselves using informal speech, often interrupting each other, hesitating, rephrasing and repeating themselves. Barnes (1976) argues that talking is essential to learning and lays particular emphasis on the value of talk among children when no adult authority is present.

When working on the tasks the children had to question, instruct and inform one another. Such processes have been defined as 'functions' by Tough (1976), Halliday (1978) and McCarthy (1991). It was interesting to observe the ways in which children tried to convey the exact meanings of the clues and problems to each other. At times they read words incorrectly and related them to previously known words – for example the word 'terrain' was read as 'train'. This affected the meaning of the word and the children's understanding of the clue but what it did not affect was the accomplishment of the task. This was largely due to the support given by the context.

On certain occasions, teacher intervention was necessary. Generally, open-ended questions were asked such as 'What do you think you have to do then?' 'How do you think you can make it so it floats?' 'What does it sound like?' According to Tann (1991) 'questions are a useful way of helping us to understand the learning process'. They can provide immediate feedback on how the participants are thinking, as well as on what they know. The children were fully engaged in the practical aspect of the task. Their language was based around reading instructions, handling the equipment and assembling it together. As Sutton (1992) observes 'Practical experience can never speak for itself, but the words we use are necessary interpretive instruments of understanding'.

Some initial problems occurred as the children developed their skills in interpreting the clues and performing the tasks. When they read the clues they would sometimes latch onto the familiar words and immediately set off on the practical task. Intermittent interruptions by children would mean that not all the children would initially hear each clue being read. Also if a dominant reader mispronounced a word it would often be accepted by the rest of the group and they would set off on the wrong foot. These problems were soon overcome as the children, carefully directed by an adult, realised that they had to read and reread the clues to aid their understanding. Individuals, pairs and small groups would do this at intervals and it ultimately became a normal part of the task accomplishment.

The children were given the opportunity to read the clues aloud, most of which contained certain target words. At times the teacher would intervene to check on the children's understanding of a particular word. One such example is the word 'waterproof.'

'Miss, it must be water tight.'
'Miss it means that the boat must not get wet.'
'The boat must not spill, it must float.'
'Lets no water coming in.'

This shows how the children tried to understand the meaning of 'waterproof'. They drew on all their past experiences and grappled with their ideas. Yet they could not always convey their understanding clearly enough. It is important to realise that children often approach the topics in their science lessons, not with empty minds ready to be filled by the teacher, but with quite firmly held ideas of their own. Thus it is important to find out what ideas the children already had about the topic. 'Ideas which seem rational to the pupils must be taken as the starting point and ideas from the previous experience must be called upon in trying to make sense of a new experience' (Osborne and Freyberg, 1985).

The children became progressively more confident about reading the clues and making attempts to decode the more difficult items of vocabulary, such as 'buoyant', 'terrain', 'communicate'. Only sometimes did they pause to question the meaning of these words – words that had been deliberately included so that we could ascertain whether the children could work out the meanings from the context. Would they ask for clarification or would they ignore what they did not immediately understand? Usually they took the latter course of action. If they could get by with 'skipping' over the meanings, they would do so. They had an urgency to get on with the task and would not question all the word meanings unless they perceived that understanding them all was essential.

Although the language the children had difficulty with did not affect their understanding of the tasks, we must consider to what extent they learned the scientific concepts in relation to the vocabulary used. Was it appropriate for new scientific ideas and vocabulary to be introduced in this context without the help of a teacher? When the children were asked what the words in the clues meant, they were unsure about some of them. If the teacher had provided explanations of the vocabulary during the tasks then perhaps the children may have had easier access to the scientific concepts. Conversely, having an adult or teacher always providing the answers would have inhibited children from negotiating the meanings themselves.

After the work in the Forest had been completed, we decided to determine what the children understood about the tasks and whether they knew what specific items of vocabulary meant. We informally interviewed them and gave them a questionnaire to complete. The children were asked to work in pairs so that they could support each other in their thinking and in their writing. We selected key vocabulary used in the written clues and the children were told to 'Find a friend and then work out what you think these words mean. Write down your answers next to each word.' The words targeted were these:

clue, sink, solve, problem, signal, message, circuit, insulator, repeat, waterproof, buoyant, polythene, terrain, communicate, conductor, switch, language, stable, limit.

Reading their responses to selected vocabulary items confirms that children bring a wide range of experiences to support their interpretations. This can be seen in the following examples:

clue
a clue solves problems
a clue helps you solve a mystery
when you are guiding yourself
if something is hard somebody can give you a clue
find out what you have to do
when we went to the Enchanted Forest we had some clues
a clue is an idea
if you don't know your addings up you can ask your teacher who will give you a clue

sink
sink means when something drowns
when something floats and doesn't drown
if you cannot swim ask someone to help you
where you wash your hands
if something has a hole like in a ship it can sink
if you go in the water you do not come back up
doesn't float
something is heavy and sails under water
it does not float it goes down
when you go in the water and you don't come back up

solve
when you find an answer
when you guessed the question
you have to get it done and get rid of it
sorting a problem out

Trying to get it right

problem   when you can't do something
that someone says that thing is mine
when you're finding somebody
solve problems
when you have to do something and you don't know how

repeat   when you say something two times
they've said it again
when the same things happen again and again
I'm going to repeat this word again
if somebody can't listen then repeat
to copy somebody
if someone is thinking and you say the same thing

waterproof when water can go through something
when only water can go through something
when water doesn't go through
something you wear and you don't drown
when something cannot get wet through – a coat can be
waterproof
if somebody puts water on the paper it will tear
so it doesn't get wet
it does not get wet in water
water cannot go through
it will never sink
put something in the water

buoyant   (most children offered no answer)
when something happens to you
when you wear something and don't drown
when you feel like something and you do it to someone

stable   where animals live
an animals' barn
where horses and cows and sheep live
where there is lots of hay
Jesus was born in a stable
where people put their horse food
where sheep live
in a farm you have a small room

limit   how fast you know how fast – like a speed limit
where something goes fast
when you cannot go past something
you cannot go past that time
the same height
you cannot go past the limit

The written questionnaire and the discussions between a researcher and the children focused on the children's understanding of the targeted vocabulary. It was interesting to see how children defined particular words. Some children wrote that terrain was 'training people'. They were obviously associating the word with something that they already knew, even though it did not quite fit into the context.

The variety of definitions offered for 'solve' demonstrated how children may slightly misinterpret a word where we would have taken their understanding for granted. The children understood the meaning in context, but their precise definitions were not always accurate. It has been suggested that children make sense of the language in the context first and only later come to understand what each individual word means (Donaldson, 1978, Sutton,1992).

The context obviously helped the children a great deal to interpret the meaning of words in the clues. For example, despite the multiple meanings for 'sink' the children interpreted it correctly by relating it to the nature of the task and the context in which it was supplied. However, being involved in communication in a real context does not always make meaning more accessible. This was certainly the case with the homonym 'stable.' The children tended to interpret 'stable' according to their own previous experiences, rather than for its targeted meaning of stability.

The children found words such as 'buoyant', 'limit', 'insulator', 'conductor' and 'communicate' difficult to define in later discussions. Yet they had accomplished the task and gained approximate meanings of these words in the practical context. 'Buoyant' was particularly difficult for the children to interpret. Its meaning had been supported in the practical activity through juxtaposition with 'waterproof' and its relationship to floating. Most children avoided giving a written definition, but a few children offered interesting answers. They must have drawn on previous experiences in order to write 'when something happens to you'; 'when you wear something and don't drown'; 'when you feel like something and you do it to someone'. We were impressed with the sophistication of their definitions and hadn't expected children of this age, let alone our additional language learners, to have heard this meaning of 'buoyant' connected to feelings and emotions. The children were obviously becoming more confident in expressing their ideas and opinions.

The experiences in the Forest were valuable not only to the children who were involved in the project but also to the adults. The students and teachers were able to analyse their own roles as teachers. They had the opportunity to reflect on their own practice and to adopt their future planning and teaching strategies. It was difficult at first not to direct the children and not to provide them with the right answers.

Research has proven that children become accustomed to working under the direction of the teacher, at times at the expense of thinking for themselves and being proactive. The development of these children as proactive learners and decision makers was certainly evident by the end of the project. They were now analysing and evaluating the events that occurred in the Forest. They told anecdotes and gave each other advice about what to do next. This stands in direct contrast to their performance at the beginning of the project when they were asking the teacher what to do next. We had to learn to take a step back to allow the children to formulate their own hypotheses and work strategies. This was not always easy.

The children demonstrated that they could move on from the contextualised learning environment of the Forest and could discuss vocabulary and meaning in a decontextualised situation. They enjoyed engaging with the vocabulary and demonstrated their ability and desire to provide definitions. Although the written questionnaire was completed back in the classroom and the targeted vocabulary items had been in the clues, the children were not told to focus on the specific context of the Forest, so they brought a range of different interpretations to these items of vocabulary. They drew upon previous experiences as well as those gained through the activities in the Forest and provided a range of different definitions and understandings of the words.

Our research showed that we, as teachers, need to be proactive in developing children's vocabulary through empowering children's 'semantic curiosity and the confidence to share ideas about the world' (McWilliam, 1998). We realised that we need to be sharply aware of how we introduce vocabulary to children, and plan clarity of expression in our delivery. We need to stretch children's thinking about the meanings of words in different contexts. Further, we discovered the importance of negotiating word meanings with the children to develop our own understanding of how meaning works. Vocabulary development is crucial to understanding the curriculum and it is of paramount importance to establish this at primary level. By doing so, teachers will be able to provide a firm foundation for learning as the children move through the education system.

CHAPTER 4
SUPPORTING PANJABI CHILDREN'S ORAL CULTURE
AVRIL BROCK

The whole project began with the bilingual students telling the children the story of Kaliya getting lost, in both Urdu and English. When the children heard the story in their first language, they listened all the more intently. Using both languages not only enhanced the storytelling but also encouraged the children's use of their first language.

Most children in Britain who are acquiring English as an additional language will be British-born and part of the local community. The aim of education is to empower all children to reach their full potential. Bilingualism is an advantage in our international society and needs to be supported wherever possible.

Language and culture are central to family and identity. Many schools have their own policy for multicultural education, supporting the culture and language of all pupils, providing equal opportunities for all the pupils to achieve. All educators need to respond to individual children's needs, demonstrating an awareness, acceptance and consideration of children's cultural experiences and linguistic skills.

Over the last twenty years there has been a great deal of research demonstrating how the development of the first language accelerates the learning of a second. Ever since the Bullock Report of 1975, which asserted the importance of first language, schools increasingly recognise that bilingualism is an asset, an extra advantage.

Research and practice have demonstrated that the acquisition of English is most effective where first language skills are brought to bear. Some people would like to think it is fairly simple for young children, but second language acquisition researchers have documented that it is a complex process which takes place over a long time. First language acquisition begins at birth and continues through to at least the age of 12, with continuing acquisition of new vocabulary and forms of structure throughout our adult lives. Additional languages are acquired to varying degrees of proficiency, depending on the context and the amount of support.

Children use their first language at home – it is a major part of their lives, the main conduit of their thought processes. In order for a second language to be truly additional rather than a replacement, the first language needs to be maintained, encouraged and valued. Baker (1993), Blackledge (1994), Cummins (1984), Fitzpatrick (1987, 1994), Hall (1995), McWilliam (1998), Pinsent (1992), Romaine (1991) and Skutnaab-Kangas (1981) all emphasise the need for instruction to begin in the child's first language so that a strong cognitive understanding can be gained which forms the basis for academic learning. Competence in first language is a good foundation for competence in an additional language. Children need the space and opportunity to communicate with other people in their first language.

The collaborative work in the Forest was designed to develop both linguistic competence and conceptual understanding. Children are able to manifest much higher levels of cognitive performance when the task is presented in an embedded context or one that makes 'human sense' (Cummins, 1984). The tasks encouraged the children to think for themselves and to solve problems together. The problems and the written clues encouraged them to use their additional language to communicate in cognitively demanding ways.

Children often are reluctant to use their first language in a school situation. They are used to English being the medium of teaching and learning in school. They use first language in social chat and in the playground, but it is not often used or encouraged for exploring the curriculum. Bilingual students often find it difficult to get the children to discuss ideas in first language as well as in English.

Nazia, as the adult supporter in the Forest, encouraged the children to work in two languages, not only to develop their expertise as bilinguals, but also to deepen their conceptual understanding. When she coordinated a group to undertake tasks in the Forest, she made a decision to introduce the tasks in Panjabi/Urdu. She wanted them not only to feel confident in using their first language but to work collaboratively and explore the problems and concepts. She wanted to see if the children were better able to complete the tasks with more confidence.

At first the children mainly responded in English to these initiations in Panjabi/Urdu, but as the creating of the electric circuit generated interest and excitement, they quickly slipped into their first language. The children talked rapidly and confidently; they listened to each others' contributions and built upon each others' ideas. The storyline also gave a purpose to using first language and the children soon became involved in the imaginative theme. This was supported by one of the clues which asked which language the jinns would understand. The children created a circuit and Nazia then pushed the children's thinking and use of first language forward by demanding that the children create a switch that would work effectively and be a signal for communication.

It is important to encourage learners to make sense of new experiences to give them potential to apply the knowledge and language learned to other situations. The work was videoed and it was quite exciting to watch the successes of the children, both in terms of completing tasks successfully and of thinking aloud in first language.

Another student, Sara Ali, decided to use Panjabi/Urdu as the medium for storytelling to introduce the children to the work of the Forest. She began to explain her absence of the week before through spinning a tale about her 'adventures'. Sara drew the children's attention to some masks positioned in the Forest to enrich her storytelling. (The English translations are represented in Italics.)

Sara:	Right, turn around here O.K. now, tumheiñ pata tha last week ke jab mujhay upar chalnay kay liyay kaha gaya tha kya sabko samaj arahi hai.*
	(*Do you remember last week I was told to walk up there. Can you all understand?*)*
	Yes
Sara:	Mujhay jinn upar lay gaye thay, aur phirmayree wahañ kissay mulaqaat hui?
	(*The jinn took me up there and then, who, who did I meet there?*)
	Ghost – jinni jinni
Sara:	Kaun sa jinni ?
	(*Which jinni?*)
	Aladdin – Aladdin
Sara:	But Aladdin is not a jinni – wo jinni nahiñ haiñ.
	(*He is not a jinni*)

The children are familiar with the story of Aladdin and the Enchanted Lamp, a tale from the Arabian Nights in which there is a genie, an enchanted and powerful spirit, who lived in the magic lamp.

*(Extracts of the children's talk have been transliterated to make them more accessible to the reader. This was undertaken by several of the students, who brought their own interpretations to the task, but the extracts have since been uniformly transcribed by Gulrez Ali.)

	Miss Miss, I know jinni – Miss he's in Aladdin and miss he's fat.
	Yes miss he has, he has a tail – miss he has a tail Miss he has got magic.
Sara:	Right, to phir jab meiñ neechay ayee.
	(*Then when I came down.*)
	When I came down, what I didn't know, listen carefully, what I didn't know is kay wo jo jinn may ray peechay aa ay, right!
	(*That the jinni followed me!*)
	Aaahhh.
Sara:	Tumheiñ wo jinn kabhi nazar nahiñ aaiñ gay.
	(*You won't be able to see the jinni anywhere.*)
	Wo baat tak nahiñ kar saktay.
	(*He doesn't even talk.*)
	Tumhein yeh yaad rakhna hay kay wo tumheiñ chup karnay ki koshish meiñ hay acha.
	(*You will have to remember that he is trying to make you keep quiet, right.*)

Sara created a sense of magic using the atmosphere of the Forest, yet her voice sounded quite normal and matter of fact. This gave her credibility and the children began to 'believe' what she was saying. Their eyes were wide and they listened with eager anticipation. They alternated between gazing at Sara and throwing surreptitious glances around the room to peer at the masks and the models of strange animals which were positioned around the Forest.

Sara:	Aur kahañ hay wo? Aur kahañ hay wo?
	(*And where is he? And where is he?*)
	Miss there there there.
Sara:	Right, to yay waysay lag rahay haiñ,
	(*So this is how it looks*).
	That's right, to yeh aysah lag raha hay kay jaysay wo wahañ chup karkay baithay hamari batañ sun rahay haiñ.
	(*So it looks like it's sitting there quietly listening to everything we say.*)

	(Multiple excited and unintelligible responses.)
Sara:	Wo sab kuch sunn saktay haiñ.
	(*He can hear everything.*)
	To issi liyay wo wahan baithay huway haiñ – samaj aaee?
	(*This is why he is sitting there- do you understand?*)
	Yeh jisko jinn kehtay haiñ.
	(*The so called jinni.*)
:	Miss they are trying to pretend.
Sara:	Pretend kar rahay haiñ aur wo chup bhi haiñ.
	(*They are pretending, and they are quiet as well.*)
	Samjhay? (*Understand?*) Right.
Sara:	Right, phir jo huwa wo yay tha.
	(*Right then what happened is that?*)
	Yay kya hai jo jinn ka hay.
	(*This is, what is this that belongs to the jinni?*)
	Machlian.
	(*Fishes*)
Sara:	Machlian, (*fish*) those are animals, phir jab main neechay aarahi thi, phir jab main neechay aarahi thi, toe yay janwar sab mayray peechay aa ay thay.
	(*Then when I was coming down, when I was coming down the animals followed me.*)
	Miss!

It is interesting that Sara returned to using mainly English to direct and teach the children. This pattern is one repeated often by bilingual students, perhaps because English seems to them to be the language to use for giving instructions.

Sara:	And now to Kaliya; we have to find Kaliya. You've got to listen very carefully. OK. Right what I want you to do is to do a task, like we did last week.
	OK. Miss.
Sara:	To do what the jinns want, they want a problem solved, a task.
	Oh, oh yes.
	(Reading) Well last week you did very well, but now there is even more story to tell. The key has gone missing yet again could you search for a clue around this
	...

As the children started to read the clues and perform the tasks, there were several instances where they demonstrated their belief in the jinns. They

Yusef (11 years) views the jinns as evil

This jinn, drawn by an eight year old boy, is male, evil and can fly
around – the lines at the bottom of his feet represent flying.

accepted them as part of the process and entered into the spirit of the story,
taking upon themselves the roles of problem solvers and searchers.

> Jinni, jinni, tell us how to fix this.
> Miss, Kaliya isn't even over there.
> Miss it won't come on.

Doubt creeps in when success is elusive. The adult prompts the children,
reminding them of the purpose of the tasks. She continually embeds the
problem in the story culture which keeps them on task and stimulated to
want to communicate with the jinns.

> Do you think they are watching us?
> They're watching us but they can't talk to us.
> We have to signal to them don't we? How do we have to signal
> to them?
> We have to light up a bulb. So they understand. We have to
> make a language.

Do you just have to light it up? What does it say on that clue?
What do we have to make the bulb do?
That is a message. You've got to have a bulb. So then you can
tell them in their language to go back.

The children use logical reasoning to try to work out what to do as they
begin to think for themselves. They relate the task of making the circuit
with the need to communicate with the jinns in order to rescue Kaliya. The
strength of electricity is considered and the effect of a shock or surge of
power may have on the jinns. The children are developing the concepts of

This was drawn by a ten year old girl. The Jinn is female, good and beautiful,
in fact rather fairy like.

cause and effect, using real life situations and relating them to the imaginative context. The children build on each others' ideas and use scientific awareness alongside the storytelling theme. They are totally involved in the task in hand.

> There's too much. You can't go near them. They can't touch or anything they can't speak. There is one over there.
> Why don't we make it big enough miss? It goes to all of them.
> Miss, they might get an electric shock.

This jinn, female and good, was drawn by a boy of 8.

Do we want to get to that? What do you think? Don't you think that might make them angry?

What's this; what's this? They might go even stronger with the electric shock.
What is that black thing?
We need to make a circuit. I know how to make a circuit, I've already made one.

The adult now begins to take control and withdraws the children from the Forest. However they are still engaged in developing the story line. Time is up. The children had succeeded in collaborating, in creating an electric cir-

A boy aged 10 drew this male, evil jinn, who appears to be like the devil Shaytan, who was repelled from heaven for disobeying Allah.

cuit and a switch to send the message. As no answer was forthcoming until further resources could be developed, the children needed to be removed from the Forest. A return to the story mode enabled this to be undertaken successfully.

> I think we need to hurry up because I can see some people looking at us. Since that creature got hurt they've been giving us funny stares. You better hurry up to send the message and get out of here before something happens.

After the work in the Forest (hut in playground!) Sara returned to the school to talk to the children about their story experiences at home. They relayed that they were constantly told stories by other members of their family and they stated that the storytellers used their first language, some-times dual language, but rarely English alone. They began to tell her stories

A 7 year old girl's drawing of a male, evil jinn.

that they were familiar with from home and relayed a wealth of personal oral culture. Several of these stories were about jinns, which are a part of South Asian culture and so familiar to many of the children involved in the project. The children had different levels of credibility about the tales and legends, which were part of their imagination. There is no single word in English for jinn and the nearest definition is perhaps as 'unseen creatures'. The world of the jinns and the stories told about them are full of secrets, magic and wonder.

The responses of the children to the oral storytelling highlight how the children's story experiences come through their first language. Storytelling is a powerful context for the development of the value of the spoken word. There is power in the narrative mode, which shapes experiences and creates meaning. Stories can provide tremendous stimulus for spoken language, when pupils are encouraged to retell them in their own words and, of course, their first language (Pinsent, 1992). Repetition of stories and key vocabulary are important aspects of language learning; if the same words are given frequently and at short intervals, they rapidly become fixed in memory (Gross, 1992). Stories are everywhere – they are part of home, current events, school, and they help us make sense of our world and build our personal identity and have an important role in all our lives. Rosen (1984) notes how this is particularly so for young children who live, think and talk though a story structure – real or invented – and interpret their world through a story.

Thanks to Maggie Power's interest and efforts, the children already had an environment which promoted storytelling. Sara asked Maggie about story and drama in the classroom and quoted part of her interview with her in her final dissertation. Maggie believes that

> It is important to empower children, that they should go home from school having a story in their head. They can then tell and share the story both in their first language and in English with family and people in their community.

Maggie promotes oral storytelling by using certain strategies: teacher-in-role and hot seating, examining different versions of similar stories, creating alternative endings, but mainly just by telling stories – to which the children listen attentively. The children benefit from the teacher's knowledge of their linguistic capabilities and experiences and the way she structures the storytelling accordingly. The children listen and feed the language back, and the structures and concepts appear in their stories, told and written – all signs that they have retained the vocabulary of the story. Maggie thinks it vital to tell stories that cater for bilingual children and their cultures. The children need to see themselves in the stories as heroes and heroines. It is important that we, as teachers, choose role models that have strong women in them. Oral storytelling has potential for interacting with the children She values it as a group activity which can be more dramatic and interesting than reading a book.

Once the first phase of the research project was completed and we began to analyse and reflect upon the transcripts of the children's language, this spin-off of the children's imaginative story-telling became an intriguing new focus. A couple of months later, I decided to return to the children involved in the project and examine the children's story-telling culture. Did they have powerful personal imaginative lives, developed in the context of family? As the adult involved I initiated but then, instead of directing, encouraged the discourse of the children to develop ideas or to clarify understanding as an active listening partner. Most of the questions were open and I had no fixed expectations of the children's responses. They were eager to return to the Forest and the first three children – Matloob, Fatima, Shazia – responded eagerly to my initial probing.

> Come and sit down and we'll do some storytelling. You were right. Until we came into this Forest, I had never heard of jinns before.
> Miss, just now when Shazia and I were looking she went away and she saw a jinn. A jinn peeped through that hole.
> Don't tell them.
> I saw them looking.
> Do you have dreams about them?
> I have good dreams about chocolate.
> I have bad dreams about jinns
> Every jinn is bad; why they are ghosts!
> They're ghosts?

I use this approach many times throughout the discussions, repeating children's statements as questions and so eliciting further explanation. This gave the children control and allowed them to be the experts in the discussions. We begin to talk about belief and they demonstrate the ability to engage in philosophical discussions. The stories are shown to be vivid and rooted in the culture of home.

> And your dad told you this, so your dad believes in jinns then does he?

> Miss, all my family knows about them, they believe in them. You
> should always believe about jinns then the jinns don't hurt you.
> They're real stories. They're real stories that I told you now.

The children talked animatedly about stories they had seen on television
and offered long descriptions about ghost stories. They used the environment of the Forest to help illustrate their discussions. This led to a lively
discussion exploring the theme of good and bad.

> Like that thing on the head (points to a mask in the Forest) and
> they have the same thing like that, except for their feet, they
> haven't got feet and do you know they've got a body like us and
> they can't wear clothes and their bodies have got a belt over
> there and they've got a ponytail over there.
> Miss, looks like in Aladdin.
> Sometimes jinns are good and sometimes they're bad.
> Do you know in Pakistan they are mostly bad. There are giants.
> There are more here than in Pakistan.
> Who told you that?
> My mum.
> Miss, if you be kind to him he will be kind to you, except for bad
> jinn, but if you be kind to bad jinn he will still be bad to you.
> In Pakistan there are more than here; in hot countries they come
> most.
> In Pakistan there are big giants miss.
> As if!
> As if!
> There are.
> I think that's the radiator.

A noise in the room makes all the children turn around a little nervously –
after all we are talking about jinns in the middle of the Enchanted Forest!
The children relate to questions about 'What will happen?' as a realistic
problem. They answer promptly and talk about the need for protection.
They are enjoying the 'unknown'.

> If you lie down among the ... nothing will happen to you
> I've got the leaf, I've got the leaf and nothing will happen to me. If
> a jinn comes up to me I've got the gold.

This philosophical discussion about reality and fantasy could have been
taken further. It is difficult to determine what the children really believe or
disbelieve, but the actual answer hardly matters – more important are the
discussions and debates that could arise. The Forest environment provides
an atmosphere that enables free discussion.

> It was just pretend.

Outside the room the children deny the storytelling that has just gone on. Their passionate discussions inside, that seemed so real and were told with such credibility are now dismissed as only pretend. Then Gulsharan, Asif and Sheeryn joined me in the Forest.

> Miss that's in our language.
> Jinn? What does it mean?
> Miss it means a ghost.
> Do you know stories about jinns?
> Yeah.
> Everybody be scared when they hear the ghost.
> I wrote story about a jinn.
> Miss, once there was a girl she met a jinn in the woods and the jinn took her somewhere in the woods.
> I know that story.
> And then they came to look for her and no one could find her and they looked everywhere for her and they never found her, nobody could find her, and someone like a fairy or something and the fairy said something to her.
> In her dreams.
> She said something in her dreams.
> What happened to her?
> Then in the morning when she woke ...
> How do you both know the same story? Did your mother tell you the story?
> No my cousin; we're cousins!
> Ah, so your mum told you both the story. Is it your mum? Does she tell you lots of stories?
> Yes, when I go to bed.

Here is further evidence of a rich storytelling culture in the home environment that passes down extended families. These children can build upon these experiences and share them with others. Storytelling is a rich part of the bedtime experience for these children and what better time to tell stories that may be a little frightening – evening provides and creates an atmospheric context.

> Miss, the room is different, some things are changed. When we came first that was there and now that isn't there.
> Why has this tree fallen down?
> The jinn!
> The jinns have moved it.

The children now perceive that the jinns are responsible for anything that happens in the Forest. The imaginative context is having an effect and stimulating their thinking. The transcripts of the discourse undertaken in the Forest demonstrate the confidence of the children when they are telling stories on a familiar cultural theme. They are eager to participate and control the discourse for a prolonged period, with only a little prompting from an adult.

> How can you tell what's true and what's a story?
> When my mum tells them.
> Does your dad know about the jinns?
> Yes.
> Do they all tell you stories then?
> My mum told me a story about it. There was a girl goes to the woods and finds a teddy bear.
> Yeah and the teddy bear ...
>
> This girl has grey hair and when she goes to the woods she finds the next teddy bear she thinks ... then there is a thing grabbing her and then took her to somewhere and then the ... woman took her somewhere ... this is a true story. I know and they keep finding her and this prophet told the mum that there is this teddy bear and where's it gone and they keep looking for the teddy bear and they can't find it and where's it gone. Then somebody else took a teddy bear ...

What is true or not true could have been debated further. Does it depend on the credibility of the story or on the power of the narrator? It was an ideal time to philosophise about reality and fantasy. Fisher (1990) states that productive discussion does not happen without establishing an appropriate physical environment to encourage talk. The session needs to be interesting and fruitful, there should be few external distractions, the children should be able to hear each other clearly, dialogue should occur in a stress-free setting. Fisher gives examples of children engaging in talk about deep and puzzling questions, in particular what is real and what isn't. In the Enchanted Forest the children were confident and interested, and the informal atmosphere generated a free flow of ideas. Children often listen to other children more attentively than to the teacher. At times the children interrupted one another or several talked at once, but this was only because their ideas burgeoned and needed expressing. Children are receptive and they do not lack the ability to discuss philosophical matters only the opportunity.

The children speculated about dreams, what is real and unreal, what would happen if, what belongs to story and what might really exist.

When the children told their stories about the jinns they became expansive and used elaborate gestures and facial expressions. They talked seriously with a strength of opinion to convince you to believe their assertions. They were both actors and information givers, with myself as the audience, the adult who wanted explanations and who was empowering them in their roles as experts. Heathcote (in Wagner, 1976) stresses the importance of children assuming the mantle of the expert to enable them to take control, express their views and develop the dramatic experience.

> Miss, in Pakistan. It's worst. I'm scared.
> In Pakistan there is a big forest near my mum's house and she would not let me go in.

It is evident that stories about or from Pakistan provide rich material for their imaginations and the distance and history adds to their excitement. However, there is also a lively storytelling culture operating in the playground.

> Miss, I am scared in toilets every day.
> I quickly go in and walk out.
> Miss, a lot of people are saying that when we go to the toilet that when you put the tap on and when you open it you say blue baby and it comes out.
> You say blue baby out and it comes out.
> You say blue baby, blue baby, blue baby.
> It's a true story.
> It's a true story? At these toilets?
> Some kids say that in the girls' toilets when we have two weeks holidays and he says that there is a little baby.
> Miss, there can't be a blue baby coming out of the tap.
> Yes there can.
> There can, why the jinns can be everywhere, they can take something from the shop, they can do anything.

The school was being redeveloped and was based in terrapins in a large playground. The children had to access the toilets by crossing from their classroom terrapin and would probably go alone during lesson time. They were convinced of the reality of the 'blue baby'. These stories originated from a picture of a small blue genie that was stuck above the taps of the sinks in the girls' toilets. In reality it is a symbol referring to the water shortage of 1996. This brings back memories from my own childhood, when my imagination transformed the shadows on the ceiling into different forms and beings.

Marc Armitage (1998), an independent consultant who undertakes play audits in school playgrounds, demonstrated that alongside the traditional ball, chase, free play and structured games, a majority of playgrounds have particular myths that appear throughout the UK. Most playgrounds have areas with nooks, crannies and dark aspects, which children turn into witches' dens, castles, dungeons, stewpots and there is often the myth of the 'white lady' who hides in the toilets. Many adults at the CECTYL conference in Sheffield, September 1998, could remember similar ghosts and spooky characters who inhabited the toilet blocks in their childhood. The last cubicle of the toilets was always a scary place! These myths and cultures are passed on from year group to year group, with a remarkable consistency from to school to school. Childhood is awash with myths and these local and cultural traditions still prevail today. Children draw on their oral traditions in the negotiation of their everyday relationships, forming their personal identities.

Hislam in Moyles (1996) suggests that adults should try 'trawling back through personal repertoire to see how evocative people, places and past events' can be in developing experiences. These can form the basis of a personal storytelling culture, which is further enhanced through cultural fables and tales. Firmly rooted in oral culture, they need to be explored through dialogue and by building upon the experiences of others. Family stories uphold tradition in an oral mode and carry anecdotes and tales from one generation to the next.

A culture provides connecting links for children and offers a scaffolding of understanding. Children, like adults, learn through the mediation of others. Cultural experiences are powerful and enable us to interpret the world and its social conventions. Parents and grandparents are significant mediators for children in structuring their cultural knowledge and heritage and relating these to their experiences of the world around them. Different cultures make meaning in different ways – the experiences children bring to the classroom are formed in social learning from the adults where children live and develop. Community cultures are diverse and all children have vast experience of different cultural values and ideologies (Luke and Kale in Gregory, 1997).

Heath (1983) and Wells (1987) both revealed through their research that many children have experienced thousands of story experiences in the home environment prior to attending school. Young children learn much more language out of rather than in the formal life of school. Shirley Brice Heath's research has examined the complex patterns of children's language use in and out of the classroom situation, exploring the cultural implications for children's language and learning. She determined that language learning may be linked to particular relationships, for example with grand-

To   avril

Thank you very much for letting as going to the forest. We have found Khaliya and he was very happy. Today you mist the day when we found khaliya. We followed the foot steps and we found a big faint Key. We put it in the door and Khaliya came out. We had clues to solve. We are glad he has not died.

Love from
            Harvinder Gill

parents, and that certain genres of language functions are loaded within these relationships e.g. stories, anecdotes, sayings. These affect children's notions of identity, their sense of style, personality and roles, which in turn have a strong impact on their confidence. At home adults may well lead discussions with the children, while constantly cooperating with them, understanding and valuing their contributions. Parents prepare the children for life, for a place within their culture. They mould their religious and cultural beliefs.

We need to gain an awareness of the wealth of traditional tales, beliefs and customs experienced by children. And children are eager to demonstrate their expertise to a listening adult. Fox (1995 in Campbell) states that parents make a significant contribution and that teachers need to be aware of the storytelling taking place at home. In particular teachers should take heed that parents have the ability to develop their children's imaginative skills, particularly in relating experiences to cultural identity, to myths, to religious expression and to philosophical thinking. Cramer (1997) demonstrates how a collection of children's own stories can be one of the most powerful contexts for language and learning that teachers can use.

On the other hand teachers may feel that children are inadequately prepared by their families for life in school (Volk, 1997). We need to be more aware of the teaching and learning that goes on in the home environment and to

> To Avril
>
> Thankyou very much for taking us in the forest. We found Kalia I'll tell you how we found him. When my group went We found the first clue it said follow the dogs step. the second clue was go and find the map and you will find the third clue was go under the castle. the third clue was go under the tunnel We went under the tunnie. We found a golden key in a box we found the fourth clue and it said if you want to free kalia so be careful. We read the fifth clue and it said this will tell you how to free kalia find a door were this key will fit so We found the door were the key fited and kalia and a man come out.
> thankyou very much.
>
> Love from Saima Iqbal.

build on the resulting competences in school. There are differences that need to be ironed out, facilitating learning which involves school, home and cultural expectations. In the classroom, children need to move language into different domains while using their existing frames of reference to seek information and ask questions. Children need to be able to be critical and to reflect, but also to build on their experiences to think ahead about what to do about their work. Heath (NALDIC conference, 1998) promoted the embeddedness of children in their sense of work. When they have purposeful situations, they can use vocabulary in context, play roles that produce a product and they speak as a character in role. Transmitting knowledge to others is the most effective way of language learning. Teaching strategies that promote performance, problem posing, assessment and critique will support new language use, help children to take risks and draw upon different brain capacities.

The children's discussions and stories in the Forest show how their cultural storying experiences can be a powerful path into collaborative discourse upon a familiar theme, in this case linking the worlds of reality and folk tale. It is evident that children do not gain such experiences only in their early years and that they are a part of everyday home life. In families they may take the form of bedtime tales, religious beliefs, jokes and teasing, but they are a living and constant part of oral culture. The children involved in our project demonstrated their capacity to discuss ideas and stories seriously. They expressed themselves clearly and confidently. They could be assertive and act as experts, building upon family and cultural experiences. They could philosophise when asked to explain or conjecture – relating the real to the unreal. They built upon their own story experiences and listened with attention to other children's explanations, identifying key points in the discussions. It is evident that children are capable of directing and controlling discourse in a serious manner with minimal input from an adult. As teachers, we should surely seek to exploit this skill to the full.

Bilingual learners need an environment where they can practise, explore, think and talk aloud. They need opportunities to talk in and beyond practical activities. They need to be able to make mistakes and feel that their attempts and opinions are taken seriously. They need to feel that their own language, culture and family are respected. Self esteem, attitudes, social and emotional well being are key aspects for successful learning to occur. Culture, identity, knowledge, experience and language are all closely interwoven. Family and community members are vital to the educational success of young children. Children need to see their own language, religious beliefs, lifestyles and histories recognised and valued. As teachers we should encourage children to take on the role of the 'experts' in story-telling, providing cultural information and demonstrating their capability to work in more than one language. We can learn about their knowledge, background and expertise and provide important stepping stones to their further development and learning.

CHAPTER 5
DEVELOPING CHILDREN'S CONFIDENCE IN SPEAKING THEIR FIRST AND SECOND LANGUAGES THROUGH DRAMA
STUDENTS' ACCOUNTS

1 ENCOURAGING PUPILS TO SUSPEND BELIEF

HILARY RIDER AND NOREEN HUSSAIN

We worked on a regular basis with eight reception children, seven of whom were learning English as an additional language. The Forest could be used for other areas of the curriculum but we found the environment particularly conducive to developing drama and language. Our overall aim was to develop the use of language in both English and the children's first language, Panjabi/Urdu. This approach promotes respect for all languages and cultures and broadens the children's experience in acquiring new language (Bruce, 1987). We always told stories in Panjabi/Urdu first, with Hilary copying what Noreen said so that the children's first language was obviously valued.

Tough (1979) found that if they are given the opportunities, children aged 3 to 5 are able to maintain their own interests, report on present experiences, direct their own and other's actions and make requests to satisfy their pleasure and comfort. The eight children had already achieved this level of linguistic competence in English as well as in their first language. Language is embedded in everyday situations and we tried to create situations which would allow the children to extend their use of language.

We wanted to learn more about children's language development and become more confident about teaching them drama. We were aware that drama helped to develop children's imagination and language but not sure how to approach it. We had used elements of drama in role-play situations and performance of familiar stories e.g. 'Goldilocks and the Three Bears', 'The Three Little Pigs' etc... but as Woolland (1993) remarks ... 'one of the problems of acting out a well-known story is that the children already know how it ends'.

As language students we wanted story to be a part of the drama lessons and believed that narrative would strongly influence the children's responses. Story is used as a vehicle for many areas of learning and we felt it would develop an understanding of word meanings as well as the language of books. Heathcote (1995) refers to the discovery of word meanings on a page as a 'distilled human experience' and asserts that children who have made the discovery have 'cracked the code'. Those who have yet to make the discovery can be helped through drama... 'readers give life to text and in this sense, reading is akin to role-playing in drama' (Heathcote and Bolton 1995).

Drama assists the development of speaking and listening and promotes active use of a variety language functions and it is a subject which crosses all curriculum areas. It is not a National Curriculum subject but it is integrated throughout the subjects in the attainment targets and, we believe, should be incorporated in all termly plans. Drama allows children to participate equally and can motivate them to learn. Difficult issues can be raised and feelings addressed in a non-threatening manner, giving children the opportunity to express their innermost thoughts and feelings.

Young children enjoy acting out, miming and role-play and most find that they can slip easily into imaginative situations. We found that actively involving ourselves in the drama process assisted the children's journey into fantasy and enabled them to use appropriate language which we had targeted in our planning. As drama teaching novices we too were on a learning curve and early sessions were sometimes hindered by our expectations. We found ourselves instructing the group and their responses were frustrated by our prescriptiveness. Eventually, we learned to 'go with the flow,' building on their interests and encouraging them to talk. In this section we describe and justify our activities, analyse the children's responses and make observations regarding their language achievements.

The National Curriculum programme of study for speaking and listening requires children to be given opportunities to:

> tell real and imagined stories
> explore, develop and clarify ideas
> describe events and experiences.

Extension of vocabulary should include understanding what words mean in different contexts, words with similar or opposite meanings and characteristic storytelling language. We promoted situations which enabled the children to express and explore feelings. Our aims were

- to encourage children to become actively involved in the drama work and enjoy themselves
- to create an atmosphere where children would feel relaxed using their first languages
- to positively encourage the use of both English and first languages
- to build confidence and self-esteem
- to develop the children's understanding of the written word
- to develop storytelling skills
- to develop speaking and listening skills
- to promote imagination and collaboration
- to explore feelings and key issues raised
- to acknowledge each other's languages with respect.

The children were chosen by the class teacher, who challenged us with a mixed ability group, who also ranged from the very shy to the very confident. The teacher chose the children whom she thought would most benefit from the drama experience. Their first languages were Gujerati, Panjabi/ Urdu and English and they brought a variety of linguistic experiences to the classroom and so were an asset and resource in themselves.

The children were reluctant to speak in their first language. They were amused when Noreen spoke in Panjabi/Urdu, but this was perhaps because they were not used to hearing the language in school. Other reasons for not using their first language could be lack of confidence – people might make fun of them, teachers not encouraging them to use it, parents also discouraging them from using their first language at school. We wanted to encourage the children to use their own language because we agree with Pinsent (1992).that 'Bilingualism can become a force in their development and a real benefit to their overall academic and intellectual progress'.

We planned various activities, ranging from introductory circle games to acting out a story. At first we concentrated on providing simple activities to help the group feel comfortable, as we had not worked with them before. We began with circle games. Neelands (1984) regards drama as a development from children's play (games) and as using the same imaginative ability and self-control. There are many advantages to using games, as they contain dramatic elements such as narrative, ritual and role-play which would prepare the way for further drama work. The terms of a 'drama contract' are similar to the rules of a game. By the end of the first session when the children introduced themselves, they began to feel that it was alright to speak in their first language. Other activities required them to listen closely to what their peers said or what we told them to do.

In the next session we involved the children as narrators and actors. Clear verbal indications were given to distinguish between fantasy and real life. The children had recently heard the story of 'Jack and the Beanstalk'. The Enchanted Forest became the backdrop for their version of the story. They had to use listening skills to tell the story in sequence. Intervention by the adults in the form of questioning encouraged them to think about someone less fortunate than themselves and they began to explore and relate to how others felt. We initiated the drama in role and they were to improvise assuming the role of Jack which they did happily.

We suddenly realised we were telling the children what to do and making all the decisions for them. 'If we're teaching maths we might demonstrate how calculations are done, but we can't expect children to learn how to do them if we do all the sums in their workbooks' (Woolland, 1993).

Each session began with circle time, offering opportunity for reflection on previous work. As Woolland (1993) observes: 'It is largely through reflection that children learn to value what they are doing'. Our analysis of the teacher's role had made us aware of the importance of reflection and throughout the remainder of the sessions we often paused in the drama to reflect with the children.

When we enacted the story of 'Jack and the Beanstalk', one of us had to play the Mother because all the boys refused a female role. In a later session the children revisited the top of the beanstalk. The children had transformed the Enchanted Forest into 'Bradford Kingdom' and now they participated freely, thanks to our reformed strategies and language use. The response in this lesson was much improved, their imagination and actions producing metaphorical language. The group discovered a castle and decided a witch lived there – as opposed to the giant. A pause at this point elicited a change from the stereotypical wicked witch into a kind-hearted one. In role and using naturalistic dialogue, the adult explained that she had lost her magic powers. The status of the adult role was low at this point and needed the children's help. The response was immediate – the group were up on their feet searching for the lost powers. Using imagination and symbolism, they brought her the items they found and explained their magic powers. They chose their vocabulary carefully to express their ideas. The session closed with a discussion of how a story can be told in so many ways. The group were able to recall their experiences, telling the story as they had performed it, each giving their own interpretations, each using their chosen vocabulary in English and their first language, but all feeling a sense of achievement.

In the final session we used a wooden key to set the scene. Belief is crucial to drama and using concrete objects as a starting point '...arrests the attention of the group and helps their belief...' (Wagner citing Heathcote, 1976). Creating belief began when Hilary came alone to collect the group from their classroom. Noreen was already in the castle in the Enchanted Forest. The group asked where Mrs Hussain was and were told she was ill – what Heathcote refers to as the one big lie. After circle time the children were allowed to explore the Kingdom which had been discussed in reflection time. Hilary slowed the pace down to create a tension which would allow the group to learn from their actions. The narrative kept the children involved in the plot and the strategy was used to examine what was happening in their story, which they had modified from the version they heard before ever going into the Enchanted Forest. Instead of a dog, it was a girl who could only speak Panjabi/Urdu who had been lost. When they found her (a student in role), they needed to draw upon previous experience and their linguistic skills to establish what was happening and what needed to be done. The children's bilingual skills were brought to the fore. Various roles were adopted in their quest to return the lost girl to her rightful home and specific registers were employed. The children had assumed Heathcote's 'mantle of the expert'. Their roles included –

a magician, who with the key (now made magic by imagination) could unlock the mystery

a policeman/policewoman who telephoned for help

a taxi driver who knew exactly where to take the lost girl in order to reunite her with her parents.

In a hot-seating session, these experts informed us of their contribution to returning the lost girl to her home. The session was so successful that the group were reluctant to be brought back to reality. As emergent teachers of drama, we found this immensely exciting and rewarding.

Our knowledge of the value of using and incorporating first language in school enabled us to work patiently with the children. They grew in skill and confidence over time, as they realised how valuable they and their home language were to us. The experience has made us shift our new emphasis on our teaching strategies, affirming how effective drama is in the delivery of language education. Although we had only a short time to learn the 'craft' of drama teaching we found the experience hugely rewarding.

Here is an acrostic poem by children in Year 4 Grange Road First School, that reflects some of the children's ideas developed in our class.

The Enchanted Forest

Elephants squirting water.
Narrow paths.
Chasing animals.
Hairy spiders hanging on webs.
Ants creeping on the floor.
Never ending story.
Tigers roaring.
Explore footprints.
Dogs lost.

Forgotten worries.
Overhanging trees.
Raining forest.
Eveil empire.
Snakes slide and slither.
Timeless days.

2. ROLE-PLAY USING 'PETER AND THE WOLF'

MANORMA DASS AND BAKSHO KAUR

We undertook drama work in the Enchanted Forest with seven 5 or 6 year olds. Our main aim was to encourage the development of speaking and listening skills by promoting communication and co-operation with others. We hoped that if the children were encouraged to use their first language, they would develop confidence in expressing their thoughts and feelings in a relaxed atmosphere. Also, we hoped that their imagination and vocabulary would grow as a result of the drama work in which they participated. The National Curriculum Programme of Study for Speaking and Listening includes the statement that 'pupils should be encouraged to participate in drama activities ... where they can use language appropriately in a role or situation'.

Drama enables children to learn about the past, explore literature and music and also promotes understanding of themselves and those around them. Because of its usefulness in language development and in other areas of the school curriculum, drama is referred to as an important 'learning tool'. As language students, we were eager to find out for ourselves how children's participation in the drama activities helped to promote their language development. We had five one hour sessions with the children over a five week period.

We chose the story of 'Peter and The Wolf' because it had a similar setting to a forest. Warren (1992) suggests that when planning drama for young children, using a story 'is an excellent place to begin'. Our main aim was to work in partnership with the children, with all of us having equal status, so as to create an atmosphere where children would talk freely and creatively. Confident talk develops in a climate where children feel able to make mistakes, be tentative and 'think aloud' without being judged. We needed to provide an environment which would foster children's talk and tried our hardest to achieve this.

During each session, one of us took observational notes of children's responses and we recorded every session so that we could assess children's language and see if it developed over the weeks. Photographs captured some of the imaginative roles in which they were engaged and were a resource for later reflection and assessment.

In the first lesson, we let the children explore the Enchanted Forest. We encouraged them to talk about how they felt once they were inside this mysterious place, but instead they commented on the things they could see: for example, 'there's fish', 'there's trees' and 'I've seen lions'. They showed confidence in labelling and describing things in the Forest but they needed to be moved forward to develop empathy, prediction and appreciation, as well as comparison and self-expression. We encouraged children to talk about some of the animals which might live in the Forest. One child pointed to the moon when asked to think of an animal, suggesting that perhaps he did not have a fully developed concept of animals and had assumed that the moon belonged to this category because it was present in the Forest. So we helped him explore the meaning of this concept by discussing it in both English and Panjabi/Urdu. The children then each chose an animal to imitate and we engaged in imaginative play.

Some of the children copied each other rather than trying to think of other animals, so made little use of their imaginations. We intervened and encouraged children to think about how different animals move and the noises they make. We asked questions such as 'How do you think you could have made your animal seem more real?' 'Could you try making your movements taller or heavier?' According to Readman and Lamont (1996), by intervening teachers can 'create structures which challenge children, as well as offering them security and support'. Children who were shy and inhibited were encouraged to talk about the distinguishable characteristics of some animals, rather than imitating them.

After the initial evaluation of our first activity and assessment of the children's responses, we decided that the children needed practice in speaking and listening to each other. They also needed purposeful communicative experiences which would develop a wider range of vocabulary in English. We also intended gradually to develop the children's creativity and imagination.

So we decided that in the second session the children should listen to 'Peter and the Wolf' on tape. The characters in the story are represented by different musical instruments, so the children listening had to concentrate carefully. As the story did not provide any description of the characters, children were engaged in imaginative thought, whereby they were having to build a picture of each character and think about their different features and their body movements.

Three of the children found listening difficult. As soon as the tape started playing, two of the boys began to talk about other things and one girl started moving around the room away from the group. The tape was turned off and children were reminded of the importance of listening and sitting still and not spoiling the story for those who wanted to listen. Within about five minutes of the story playing, the children were sitting quietly and totally engrossed in the tale.

Stopping the tape before reaching the end of the story and asking the children 'what do you think happened next?' allowed the children to express their ideas. Predictions such as 'the wolf eats Peter', 'Peter kills the wolf' and 'the men shoot the wolf' were enthusiastically offered. This story had helped to capture the children's attention and had stirred their imaginations and set them talking. We encouraged the bilingual children to use Panjabi/ Urdu to help them to express their ideas. They seemed to feel inhibited about using their first language in discussion, although some regularly used the occasional word when they could not think of an appropriate English word.

In the third session, children were given the opportunity to think about what they did in the one before, and most of them were able to remember the story of Peter and the Wolf. They talked about specific events in the story, for example 'Peter's Grandfather took him home because the wolf was in the forest', 'The wolf ate the duck' and 'Peter caught the wolf with a rope'. We noticed that children were now more relaxed and using longer phrases, including descriptions about particular events in the story.

The children were now enthusiastic and eager to talk about the story. We let them listen to the story once more, this time in a translated version in Panjabi/Urdu, in the hope that this would help some of them understand the events and vocabulary. They did indeed become more confident in their first language. One child described the thoughts and actions of the bird, who, as she explained in Panjabi/Urdu 'Bhairya day nal mazakh kar da see – sar day gol urr di see' – 'was playing a trick on the wolf – she was flying round his head'. Another explained that 'Bhairya nu ghusa charda see kyon kay us di dum rassi wich phasi see' – 'the Wolf was getting really mad because he couldn't get his tail out of the rope'. Children were asked to focus on one or more characters in the tale and to move around the Forest and behave like their chosen character. Our job was to guess who these characters were, whether it was 'jolly Peter', 'the big fat duck' or 'the greedy wolf'. This activity involved exploring the meanings of 'jolly,' 'fat' and 'greedy' by using expressions and movements to portray these different images of the characters successfully.

The fourth session put the children in a position where they had to explain a point of view from a stance of power in the hot seat. This enabled them to reflect on the previous sessions – Heathcote and Bolton (1995) emphasise the need for reflection in drama activities, as it helps children to acquire 'new perceptions, understanding and knowledge'. Our intention was for children to understand the motives of some of the characters in the story. We initiated hot seating after 'the wolf' came to talk to them and they wanted to take on a character themselves. According to Warren (1992) selecting characters from a story 'gives more scope for the development of drama'.

As the children defended a particular character's actions, they learned how to justify the behaviour of their characters. The child playing the Wolf was asked 'why did you eat the duck?' and 'couldn't you have eaten something else instead?'and gave replies such as 'I was hungry' and 'there wasn't anything else to eat'. It was exciting to watch this child changing his voice so that it sounded deeper – as a wolf's should. The children became more and more confident, and several of them used intonation when playing their characters.

Our role was to ask the characters in the hot seat challenging questions which encouraged them to think about their actions. The children were clearly using language to explore the nature of the different characters in the story. They were actively involved and were now asking pertinent questions. This activity promoted children's self-esteem, their ability to listen and be sensitive towards others and helped them to understand different points of view.

Our aim in the final session was for the children to explore ethical and moral issues, as well as learning to work collaboratively and make joint decisions. Noreen assumed the role of the wolf, while Hilary encouraged the children to find out why the wolf was sitting all alone and upset. We accepted the children's ideas, offering them support and discussing solutions with them. Warren (1992) highlights the importance of listening to and considering children's ideas in drama lessons. The children initiated their own questions by asking the wolf 'why are you upset?', 'are you hungry?', 'do you have to eat other animals?' and 'why can't you eat our food?'. Children then began to discuss in their group how they should help the wolf to become kinder and gentler. They were given time to think about this and they managed to solve the problem by negotiating with the wolf other ways he could get his food: 'we could get you some meat from the meat shop' and 'we could make saalan (curry) at home and bring it for you'.

In this last session children were engaged in thinking about why certain things happen and how to challenge unfair situations, related to the problems faced by the wolf and the other animals in the story. The children encountered dilemmas which led them 'to think and respond with spontaneity' (Readman and Lamont, 1996). They were very much in control of their own learning and they determined and influenced the course of the lesson.

Throughout all the sessions opportunities had been created for pupils to use different functions of language – initially limited mainly to describing and explaining. However as the sessions progressed, they used a range of language functions such as predicting, asking and answering questions, describing, reporting, explaining, justifying, discussing, elaborating, reasoning and empathising.

The use of drama in assessing children's language development proved successful. It was clear that the children initially had limited experience of working in an imaginative setting and that they found it difficult to listen to others and express themselves. However as the sessions progressed, their use of language became decidedly more imaginative and confident. This was also noted by the class teacher who commented on how the children talked enthusiastically about their experiences with others in the class and were excited at the thought of attending further sessions.

We felt that a combination of different factors contributed to the development of children's language. The environment of the Enchanted Forest and the story 'Peter and the Wolf' captured and stimulated children's imagination, enabling them to talk enthusiastically. The activities we planned interested the children and encouraged them to become interested and involved. The way we organised them into small groups created opportunities to challenge their thinking and for them to respond thoughtfully. The promotion of Panjabi/Urdu along with English, the relaxed atmosphere and our valuing of all their contributions helped to promote talk in both languages. All these factors resulted in a highly successful developments for the children involved and for both of us as novice drama teachers.

3. 'NEVER LAUGH AT BEARS' – STORY AND ROLE-PLAY
HARBANS KAUR GILL AND
MOHINDER KAUR SANDHU

We worked with four boys and two girls aged 6, all of whom spoke Panjabi/Urdu as their first language. We wanted to focus on developing their confidence in using spoken language and enhance their listening skills. We personally needed to gain experience of assessing and evaluating children's oral competence and had decided to do this through the medium of drama. We were to discover how drama can be used in the context of the Enchanted Forest.

We hoped to encourage the children to form language in appropriate ways and to recognise different forms of language. We wanted them to accept the teacher in a variety of roles and themselves to begin working in a character role.

The children had not visited the Forest before and we let them explore and respond to the environment before introducing them to a story. As it was dark and gloomy, the children were hesitant about going in. Neelam clutched my hand tightly, whispering 'Miss, I'm scared' as she pulled me backwards. The children were nervous and cautious, but eager and excited. Their expressions were startled when they went into the Forest and they moved around slowly asking questions; 'What's that?' 'Is it a snake?' 'What's that noise?' 'Shall we find out?' There was a noise in a corner and the children cried 'Miss mujeh dar lagta hai' – 'Miss I'm scared.'

We explained that there were animals in the Forest and that we needed to respect their habitat. We then introduced a discussion of animals living in the Forest and we were pleased that the children were able to use their imagination and express themselves through facial expression, body language and gesture. They used vocabulary in their first and additional languages to name animals, mime animal movements and make animal noises. We showed them a magic key and asked open questions to encourage them to think about what would be behind the door of the cave. A noise from inside the cave provoked more questions: 'Who is inside the cave?' 'Does something live in the cave?' 'Could it be a bear?' A growling noise came out of the cave and grew louder and louder, and the children moved away from the noise asking: 'Are you a friendly bear or a nasty bear?' The bear (Harbans in role) emerged and said 'I am a friendly bear. I like children'. A spate of questions followed, directed at the bear: 'Where did the bear live, what did she eat, what does she do, what is her name?'

The children were curious, interested and willing to participate. They were inquisitive and explored each area of the Forest with great enthusiasm, questioning continually: 'Who is in the castle?' 'Who lives in the castle?' 'Is it a wicked witch?' 'Is it a beautiful princess?' They called out – 'Who is in the castle?' Harbans now emerged from the castle as the Princess Transvani and the children told her that they were lost. She replied that she would take them home on the magic carpet through the Forest. All the children sat huddled together on the magic carpet and called out: 'Oh dekho darakht,' 'Hum gir ja aiñ gay,' 'Carpet noo ghut kay pakar'. They told each other to watch out for the trees, to hold onto the carpet and to hold on tight so that they didn't fall off.

Their facial expressions, their body postures and their tightly shut eyes showed that they had quickly become involved in the drama and were entering completely into the role-play. They held onto the carpet tightly, ducking their heads to pass beneath and above trees, as though they believed in the flying magic carpet. The children found it easy to enter the imaginary world and we knew that we had to enter it with them. They taught us how to suspend our disbelief and we learnt how to adopt roles to develop and vary learning opportunities so as to achieve our determined learning outcomes. By becoming fully involved with the children we found we could develop themes and also build their confidence.

During the second session we introduced the story 'Never laugh at bears' and read it in a group inside the Forest. We read the story in both Panjabi/ Urdu and English, not only so that the children could hear their first language used in the educational context, but also to deepen their understanding of the story by listening to the vocabulary and structures in both their languages. They eagerly discussed the story and the characters. Neelam stated that it was wrong to hit someone and that you would be punished by God. She discussed aspects of morality and used Panjabi/Urdu to express her view clearly and articulately. We did feel that because we had shared knowledge of language, culture and religion similar to Neelam, she felt able to speak out confidently.

The children looked upon us as role models and they communicated freely in Panjabi. We believe that we were able to develop the children's concepts and language use in both languages. Communication was fluent and expressive – we did not just translate vocabulary but were interacting and developing the children's understanding. As Blackledge (1994) observes 'if children are encouraged to use their languages at their convenience, and these languages are accorded genuine value in the classroom, it is likely that existing and new languages will develop side by side'.

At first one boy, Mudasser, did not contribute to the discussions in any language. We encouraged him to take part, speaking to him in Panjabi/ Urdu and supporting him in the group work. Neelam took on the role of interpreter: 'Miss, he will understand if I explain.' She knew about the differences in accents and dialects between the different communities and realised that she could aid his understanding. 'Thanu kee changa laga story vich?' 'Which part did you like in the story?' He replied 'Jidha bear tay rabbit larday haiñ mainu oh changa laghna hay.' 'I liked it when the bear and the rabbit were fighting.'

These bilingual children demonstrated their superiority and expertise as they analysed ambiguous sentences. Mudasser's contributions were en-hanced because of the peer tutoring and frequent prompting. His confi-dence and spoken language really developed throughout the sessions. He used resources within the drama, as when he imagined he was a bird and flicked a feather up and down saying: 'Urrja, urrja cherrah soni cheerya' – 'Fly bird, fly fly beautiful bird'. Clarke and Goods (1996) observe that 'One has only to watch young children free play to see the possibilities that exist through utilising and structuring activity of this type to help them create new perspectives and understanding about their world.'

Our original intention had been to encourage the children to 'act out' the story, but we began to realise that the strength of our sessions had been our active involvement with the children in the role-playing. We decided we needed a further stimulus to develop the drama and introduced animal masks (which we created with card and dowelling!). The masks inspired the children and helped them to express the inner feelings of their animal characters. We aimed to develop verbal and non-verbal communication and the children role-played using intonation, pitch and the level of their voices and well as gesture and body language.

The bear cried angrily in a loud voice: 'Why are you laughing at me?' and the frightened woodcutter replied in a husky voice, 'Because you are such a big bear that you are frightening a little rabbit.' According to Wells (1987) 'Certainly their experience of stories enriches the range of their imaginative play, the role they take on and the understanding they show of their characters' thoughts and feelings in the predicament in which they set them.'

In this activity the children heard and spoke utterances sequenced in a narrative form and they showed they could reconstruct the story using many of the original features. Their vocabulary became more elaborate in both languages, moving from English utterances of 'It's a bear' to 'It's a big hairy bear and it's fighting with the rabbit'. We felt that their experiences in their first language helped develop their English. 'Evidence shows that bilingual children will make greater progress in English if they know that their knowledge of their first language is valued' said the Swann Report (1985). Neelam knew something about bears, 'rhich,' and she transferred this knowledge to the role-playing in English.

In the final sessions we gave the children experiences of hot-seating so they could show individual characterisation. We demonstrated the nature of hot-seating by going into role ourselves as the rabbit and the woodcutter, encouraging the children to ask us pertinent questions. The children then selected their own characters and learned to express their animal's feelings and thoughts with a little prompting from us.

Transcript of the Hot Seating

Bear (Irfan) (roaring)	Hello children
Children	Hello Mr Bear
Salma	Ap kistera feel kar day ho?
Bear	Good
Teacher	Mr Bear, the children would like to ask you something. Are you ready children?
Neelam	Why were you fighting with the rabbit?
Bear	Main kyon lar da see? (*Why was I fighting?*)
Teacher	Rabbit day naal (*With the rabbit.*)
Bear	Mainu gusa aya see kyon kay rabbit hasda see, shala mar da see. (*It made me angry. The rabbit was jumping up and down.*)
Teacher	Oh rabbit shala mar da see (*Oh The rabbit was jumping up and down.*)
Bear	Yeh, naalain oh mainu gala kad da see (*and he was swearing at me.*)
Salma	Why do you think he was swearing?
Bear	I don't know.
Shazia	Kya aaap theek samaj day see odhay naal larna, aap ethnay baray tay rabbit very small. (*Did you think it was right fighting with the small rabbit?*)
Bear	Haañ.
Teacher	Did you think it was right for the big bear to fight with the little rabbit, children?
Children	No.
Shaista	Bear, why did you want the woodcutter's gah? (*cow*)

The children were able to justify their views. For example 'It made me angry that the rabbit was laughing and jumping up and down. Also he was swearing' (the character had not done this in the story). This child related to his previous experiences, using his imagination to develop the character. The children were now working collaboratively and appeared more confident at each session. We found that by taking on a variety of roles ourselves, questioning the children and getting them to focus on particular aspects, that we had developed the children's level of thinking and they could challenge and support their ideas.

The children felt secure and confident and were happy to participate. We evaluated and adapted our teaching strategies according to the children's needs. They code-switched in Panjabi/Urdu and English, replacing words according to their linguistic expertise. Their English language was enhanced through speaking in Panjabi/Urdu, which we supported, valued and encouraged. The class teacher described how the children's oracy skills had developed throughout the drama sessions and said that they were keen to talk about their experiences, explain and discuss their activities. They could express opinions about what they had enjoyed in the sessions. She felt that they were displaying increased confidence in speaking and listening in both their languages. We valued having this time to work with a small group of children and we felt that we accomplished our own learning objectives. It had been an enjoyable and rewarding experience for us and for the children.

4. NARRATIVE FEATURES OF CHILDREN'S ROLE-PLAY IN THE ENCHANTED FOREST

RONA HEPTON AND CLAIRE NIXON

We worked with the same two groups of six Year 3 children for one hour for each group per week for four weeks, to provide a comparison and to ensure continuity and progression. We hoped to have groups of mixed ability and gender to ensure balance within the groups, but it soon became obvious that the children in the one group were more able than the children in the other, and that levels of engagement and concentration were commensurate with this ability difference. Consequently we did adapt certain activities to their different needs. We required the children to collaborate during the drama and hoped to build up their self-esteem.

Our key interest was to determine whether narrative features would be important in the children's oral repertoire. We decided to tape the children's language and transcribe their narratives. We would also observe their interaction and how they would collaborate in role-play situations. As one of us was completely new to teaching drama, this time spent working with the children in the Forest gave us a chance to try out strategies and ideas. So we needed to plan each session carefully.

We began by brainstorming open-ended questions for the children: How did we get into this place? Where are we? What can we see/hear/touch/feel?

Who lives here? What do they look like? Why are they here? What does it look like? What is it made of? What does it do? How can we release these things? What do we need? Who are you? These questions could be targeted towards different elements of the Forest environment and the resources that we would introduce from time to time. We wanted to pass as much control of the role-play to the children, to give them dilemmas to reason through and solve and to provide tension in the drama activities. The activities we devised exploited the space and opportunity of the Enchanted Forest to develop imaginative physical and mental improvisation through drama and story. As we had limited time with the children we decided to focus our aims on the children's language development, which were:

- to use language in more varied contexts in order to develop oral fluency

- to use role-play to develop and extend children's use of language

- to develop collaborative and cooperative ways of working

- to develop the ability to communicate ideas

- to listen with growing attention.

Session one was inspired by the 'Mantle of the expert'. Heathcote (1985) in Warren (1992) advocates the transfer of power from teacher to children. We felt that establishing a contract would give the children ownership of the drama and so enhance their responses. We used the technique of the 'teacher in role', which would allow the children to take charge of the drama, in this exploratory introduction to the Forest, which was as new to the children as we were. The teacher in role should be prepared to take risks and accept the children's ideas. Warren (1992) maintains that: 'Drama demands questions to which the answer is unknown until the children provide it'.

During session two we sat in a circle to create a story. We wanted the children to feel of equal status to us. Rosen in Neelands (1992) asserts that narrative has a substantial place in the analysis of everything and that: 'stories-in-the-head ... should be given their chance to be heard'. We also discussed stories in session three, where we decided to use a published story as a starting point. Wells (1987) affirms that stories enrich children's experience with cognitive development and that vocabulary is developed as children explore words in order to discuss the story. He maintains that: 'size of vocabulary is strongly related to overall educational achievement'. Stories can provide an excellent starting point for collaborative talk.

The general structure of our session was starting point, building belief, engagement and reflection. So that the drama could achieve the maximum learning potential, we established a contract between ourselves and the children at the beginning of each session. This was to ensure that the children felt safe to commit themselves to the drama. Before the 'truth circle' activity during session three, we established a contract. We agreed that we would respect all the contributions made and that within the truth circle there were no right or wrong answers (because it was a truth circle!) and that nobody could contradict a contribution by anyone else. This was to enable the children to contribute to the drama to their full potential without any fears. We also established an 'opt-out' contract ensuring a safety net in case someone did not want to contribute. Also included was what Dorothy Heathcote describes as 'the one big lie' – (Wagner, 1976). For the drama to be successful, the children had to suspend disbelief.

Next, the children acted out the story, 'The Farmer's Gift', allowing them to convey their own interpretations of it. The 'truth circle' was used to explore the description of a character. Throughout our sessions, and in particular session four, the children were engaged in role-play, being whatever character they chose to be. This gave them freedom to do and say things that they might not do and say as themselves – they had the 'safety net' of drama and could behave as their chosen character. The language they bring to the drama is from their own experiences and this is built on by the effect of the drama situation and the immediate surroundings. Whole group improvisation and teacher-in-role is discussed in Neelands (1984) as the '... closest way of working to real experience ... often the best chance of discovering new meaning .... involves everyone simultaneously' (Neelands, 1984).

We set out the following resources before session four began: a discarded blanket, half-eaten biscuits and fruit, footprints leading to a tunnel, a treasure map, a box of treasure, a rug (the magic carpet!).

The children joined the teacher on a magic carpet to take them on a journey to ...? This was open-ended, building on suggestions offered by the children. What can we see, smell, hear as we travel through the sky? Where have we landed? What can we see to help us? Has there been anyone here before us? Are there any clues?

Our discussions and analysis are focused on sessions two and four, which drew informative responses from the children when they used a range of narrative features. During the oral storytelling in session two, each group produced finished stories that varied in content and complexity, although both group stories contained fundamental elements of 'narrative'. Toolan (1988) refers to these as 'functions' and observes that:

> Functions might be expected to consist of characters of a recognisable type (e.g. villains) and events of recognisable type (e.g. discoveries or betrayals) ... or functions which were more like relationships between characters or objects and events ... so in different stories, a function could be played by different characters of different age, class, gender or species (in Stibbs, 1991).

The children's stories contain examples of these 'functions' – the substance of narrative from time immemorial. One story has dancing skeletons (the heroes) which are threatened by a flying spider (the villain). We are further convinced of the spider's villainy when it frightens some children and makes them run away. The spider then reveals itself to be a friendly spider and unveils a magic pool (magic agent). The water makes the children's wishes come true (satisfies a lack) but also reduces a lady who has over-eaten to become so tiny (magic agent) that she is stamped on by a man (further villainy). Having done this deed, the man eats all the food and falls asleep! The children were insistent that the story ended like that, but were not forthcoming about what happens to the stamping man. Was there retribution or remorse?

Extracts from the stories created in the Forest

T – Teacher E – Ebrahim F – Fozia I – Ismail M – Meriam

T: One dark night, there was an owl hooting from the top of a tree in the Enchanted Forest (laughter and interruption from child E) And in that Forest there was a ...

E: Skeleton. He was dancing. He was playing around with his friends.

T: Who were his friends?

E: The jungle, there were elephants. (Laughter)

T: Nothing is wrong. You can say whatever you like.

E: There's a dragon and some elephants. There might be spiders.

T: There's a skeleton and a dragon?

All: There might be birds. And fish... and....

T: What were they doing?

E: They are all friends.

F: They are messing about.

T: Just messing about?

F: People might be coming into the jungle scaring them away. And after scaring them they might go to sleep ... and scaring them ... and then when they wake up in the morning they don't know they are there and they just make make a mess in the house.

(The next excerpt is from later in the story)

T: When they got to the Forest, the spider showed them a ...

I: A pool. He swam in the water.

T: Why did he want to show them the water?

The 'Princess's house'

I: It's special.

T: What was special about the water?

I: It's magic water.

T: What happens when you get in the magic water?

I: You change colour .... The magic water gives you what you wish for and the children wished for something they want, like a bike or something. They went to sea.

T: You mean 'sea' as in 'seawater'? (Ibrahim nods.)

(Meriam follows on after further input from Ibrahim.)

M: And they had some food. And a lady came and she ate all the food and she got *SO* fat (Laughter). When she went in the water she drank all the river and she got smaller. There was a man and he stamped on the lady. The lady said Help! Help! The man found the lady and the lady died. The man ate up all the food, then they put more food and the man ate all the food then he fell asleep.

The other group of children created a story about a big, friendly lion (the hero) and his friend whom he feeds and chases around. Together they go on a journey to a castle and frighten everyone there (villains). However they are not what they seem (transformation) and seek help from the princess to get a bed for the night (request). She grants their wish. The lion and his friend play a joke (villains) but a real ghost comes (real villain) and frightens everyone, even the ghostbuster (magic agent). The ghost is shooed away (happy ending and resolution).

T – Teacher A – Abdullah R – Rena

A: The lion chases the goblin and then lion chases him.

R: They went into this castle and they frightened a king and a princess and a queen and a prince and the princess and the lion said I have come from the jungle Queen and ... she has given us a cave. And the princess asked the lion what are you called and the lion said my name is Lion and the goblin said my name is Goblin. And the lion said that can I stay in your house? and then the goblin said 'Can I sleep in your house?' and the princess she said 'yes' and then they slept in a big kind of bedroom and the lion slept in a little bedroom and the goblin slept in a little bedroom. The bedroom had lots of things in it, there was flowers and telephones in it and then ...

T: Shall we let Abdullah do some more of the story? So they are all asleep in their little bedrooms, then what happens after that?

A: And then a ghost came.

T: Oh! Were they frightened by the ghost?

A: Yes. He went under a sheet and scared them all. So did the lion and the goblin.

T: Oh, the lion did? He was pretending was he? To be a ghost? Then what happened?

A: And then they went back to bed. And the real ghost came back to the princess and the princess woke up and she started screaming and the lion woke up the prince and he said there's a ghost and we should call the ghostbusters to get the ghost.

T: And then what happened?

A: They all woke up and the ghost came ... and the ghostbusters got scared.

T: They all got scared too? How did they get rid of this ghost?

The stories got quite involved and confusing at times but with so many authors, this is to be expected. The fact that both stories contain such strong narrative 'functions' confirms that children are constantly drawing upon their knowledge of story from other sources. As Fox, (1993) observes:

> To tell their stories the children use tacit knowledge, knowledge they are not aware they have, of the way narratives get told. Their knowledge is a learned part of their cultural experience and is based upon what they have heard, both spoken and written, in the past.

Moreover in the second story extract, Rena introduces a King, Queen, Princess and Prince to go with the goblin, all of them familiar characters in standard fairy tales. Rena also gets preoccupied with the size of bedrooms, working from 'big' to 'small' which suggests reference to 'Goldilocks and the Three Bears,' which one of the children had said was her favourite story. Abdullah introduces a 'ghostbuster', drawn from film and television.

In the first group, Meriam's lady's size varies with what she eats and drinks, reminiscent of Lewis Carroll's Alice in Wonderland. Other elements in this story, the spiders and birds, were to be seen in the Forest environment, and so were the lion (a mask) and the skeleton (in a painting on the wall), so it was clear that the Forest was inspiring the stories.

Both the stories contain little descriptive language about character, setting, sights and sounds. This was probably because the children were so focused on the action and the sequence of events. The teacher supported both narratives with her interventions. Her questions were about 'what happens next?' rather than 'what did she look like?' or 'how might that feel?, rather than about eliciting descriptions of characters or settings. This made us realise the importance of the teacher in directing the children's thinking. Asking a wider range of questions will extend the children's responses and is likely to produce a fuller and more holistic story. Broader aspects of language could be elicited through character building, in readiness for performance or for describing the scene when scribing the stories at a later stage.

The ways the children used language in their storytelling varied. Rena's account follows on directly from the previous speaker. She introduces a number of new characters while maintaining those already established in the narrative. She creates dialogue which she presents as direct speech e.g. 'and the goblin said 'Can I sleep in your house?' This convention is also used by Abdullah later in the story. Both children use 'and' as a connective throughout their storying, which suggests that they have not yet developed the use of varied connectives, but there may be another explanation. The nature of the storytelling activity demands that the children 'think on their feet' and it may be that Rena is using 'and' to maintain her right to continue speaking as she pours out the flood of ideas she has been bottling up while waiting for her turn.

In contrast there is a more considered response from Meriam in the first group – she also uses 'and' as a connective but later also 'when' and 'then'. There is a high frequency of complete sentences including complex ones such as 'When she went in the water she drank all the river and she got smaller.' Meriam also uses an example of direct speech: 'The lady said 'Help! Help!'" Whilst Meriam would seem to be saying much less than Rena, her language appears to indicate more complex use of grammar.

The Magic Carpet strategy adopted in Session Four demanded a good deal of speaking by the children. Analysing selected excerpts of the stories enabled us to determine the types of meaning which children express through language, the linguistic purposes drawn upon, their competence in taking turns and to look at the possible origins of their ideas. Our transcript shows Rena self-maintaining and referring to the needs of her character (who has connections to the traditional tale of Hansel and Gretel) within the present imagined experience. She is also directing and controlling the actions of the other children, threatening them in her role as wizard and projecting her character by means of self-maintaining strategies for her own protection. Rena seems to have experience of characters of this kind from listening to and reading stories and obviously enjoyed participating in the role-play.

A fascination with magic continued throughout all the children's role-play. They use their imaginations and involve both physical and imaginary resources. They readily accept the pretence of travelling to faraway places on a magic carpet. Elements of the environment of the Forest are used to develop their descriptions and connect their imaginary experiences. In the following extract the pineapple actually exists – there is a large plastic pineapple-shaped container, whereas the magic box, the key, the treasure and the suitcases are all imaginary. The children mime opening boxes, looking at treasure and packing beautiful things into the imaginary suit-cases. They report to each other and project imagined objects with which they interact in their conversations and movements. The reference to Mount Olympus show Ibrahim drawing on his reading of a history textbook about Ancient Greece. He has extracted this knowledge and applies it as he knows that you can see anything when you are flying on a magic carpet. The children are keen to keep the magic carpet experience going and the carpet lands in another jungle in India.

This is my magic wand.

This is a pigeon; this is from a peacock.

(Zena found a magic box.)

This is the key.

My dad and mum gave me this when I was small.

I found this pineapple, my beautiful pineapple, I'm going to give you something.

Yes but this man came once and said I want some treasure I said no you're unkind but I'll give all my beautiful things to you.

What happened to that man?

He went away but he came back and asked about my mum and dad.

Do you want to go back with them?

Yes, I want all my things.

(Everyone packs their things in imaginary suitcases and then they debate what they can take back and pile things on the carpet.)

This pineapple is precious.

The carpet starts moving when we ring the bell.

Abracadabra let us ride.

There's Mount Olympus.

I'm really tired.

A robber might jump on us and take the treasure.

Can I be the robber?

What can you hear? Where have we landed?

Another jungle, a jungle in India – lions, panthers, tigers, hyenas.

An adult enters and asks the children questions. She has been looking for them – where they have been? What have they been doing? The children are excited and keen to report on their experiences, as they move in and out of the role-playing situation. They talk about where they have been and the roles they have created. Although an adult was present during the magic carpet ride she let the children take control and manipulate the role-playing and storying.

Miss we landed miss, we've been on an adventure, we've been to the jungle

Who are you?

I am a princess, I came from the USA.

Is that where you have been – to America?

No, we've been to the Indian jungle and I'm not scared.

I am a princess and I'm pleased to meet you.

Put the treasure in here.

(The magic carpet is rolled away.)

Several well known fairytale/storybook characters surfaced during the session – wicked wizard, witch, princess, king, queen, robber. The children used several magical elements – a magic key, a magic feather, a magic wand and the casting of spells, as well as familiar creative elements of poison and the treasure. Taping the discourse of the role-playing in the Forest enabled us to examine the children's contributions after the event as it is difficult to assess them while being part of the drama or even when observing it. We can see that the drama has allowed the children to project their imagination and use language in situations and about characters and mystical places that everyday life does not allow.

The children were given drama experiences in the Enchanted Forest which stretched their thinking and emotions and helped to stimulate their vocabulary. This demonstrates a potential for language development in the curriculum. O'Neill et al (1990) describe the learning potential of drama as: 'The ways of working in which participants are most likely to question, accept challenges, realise implications, go beyond stereotypes and discover new depths of language as a result of their involvement, in role, within the imagined situation'.

We believe that the groups of children working in the Forest demonstrated capabilities to create group stories that contain key elements of story structure. Our next step would be to develop children's realisation that after creating oral stories in role-play they could then plan and write a story. The National Literacy Strategy contains frameworks to help children plan writing narratives, of which key aspects are setting, character, dialogue, story structure, language, narrative, point of view, genre. Frameworks for story structure include the different stages of setting, problem, conflict, complication, crisis, resolution. The children's contributions showed that they were achieving these in their role-play and would have a strong foundation for writing narrative.

Although we concentrated on oral work with the children and did no writing with them, the experiences we gave them would be valuable in developing key aspects in the National Literacy Strategy in the text level work for Year 3 regarding composition. As future teachers, we would use similar drama activities to develop the children's skills in oral storytelling with a focus on the following aspects of composition in the National Literacy Strategy:

Term 1
Develop the use of settings in the stories children write by having them

- write short descriptions of known places

- write a description in the style of a familiar story

- investigate and collect sentences/phrases for story openings and endings

- use some of these formal elements in retelling and story writing

Term 2
Children to write portraits of characters, using story text to describe behaviour and characteristics

- write a story plan for their own myth, fable or traditional tale, substituting different characters or changing the setting

- write alternative sequels to traditional stories using the same characters and settings, identifying typical phrases and expressions from story and using these to help structure the writing

Term 3

Children to discuss (i) characters' feelings; (ii) behaviour, e.g. fair or unreasonable, brave or foolish; (iii) relationships, referring to the text and making judgments.

The children demonstrated competence in turn-taking and taking control of the role-play. They could accept each other's ideas and move the drama forward, building the contributions of others. We had been worried about allowing the children to take major control of the situations but were rewarded by their total involvement and their expertise in role-playing and were able to develop the children's self-esteem by praising their contributions.

The children created a group narrative that had a cohesive form around characters and plot. We felt that we had achieved our aims, in particular by helping the children appreciate and enjoy role-play and drama, and by developing and extending their language use through collaborative and co-operative ways of working and listening to each other's ideas. The children used their growing knowledge of stories acquired by oral tradition and reading to inform their own story production. Dramatisation crystallised their language, helping them to shape their imaginative experiences and develop their story framework. Children find it so easy to engage in role-play that drama activities are almost guaranteed to be successful.

CHAPTER 6
HOW STORYTELLING AFFECTS THE STORIES CHILDREN WRITE

LAKHBIR KAUR BASSI

Story is a powerful force in our lives and pupils of all ages should experience that power regularly (Dougill, 1988)

When children heard stories while they were in the Enchanted Forest we could see from their faces that they were captivated. Wide-eyed and faces aglow, they concentrated intently on every word. They entered into the emotion and atmosphere of a world where the impossible could happen.

That the stories were told rather than read clearly impressed the children. When I think back to when I listened to stories, they seemed to have come from nowhere or, as one five year old put it, 'from out of your head'. Children are accustomed to stories being read rather than told in school and they expect them to come from books. They relate the word 'story' to the written word, just as I did when I was a child.

I remember how I, like the shoemaker, yearned for the elves to assist my mother in household chores; how like Cinderella, I could not understand the selfishness of my sisters; how like Hansel and Gretel I hoped to find a house made of chocolate and sweets. Stories remain in our memories because they engage our emotions as well as imagination. Carol Fox (1993) found that children's retelling of story came closer to the fairy tale form than to any other. Fairy and folk tales play a key role in our childhood, adolescence and adulthood. Story derives from an oral tradition whereby traditional tales were told, embellished each time and transformed. And new stories were created, some based on local events (Paley, 1981).

Oral storytelling naturally invites using hand movements and facial expressions to bring characters to life and capture the attention of the listeners. Most literate cultures seem to have moved away from the art of oral storytelling, but it is great tool for learning. Telling a story breaks down the 'isolation of the listener from the reader and their text' (Tann, 1991) although this is not to say that reading a story out aloud cannot also create a powerful imaginative experience.

Telling stories as opposed to reading them seems to have a major effect on listeners. As Jones and Buttrey (1970) observe: 'Stories are not books. They properly belong not to our tradition of print but to speech, not to our skill in reading but to our natural urge to listen and talk'. Reading a story can cause problems over the meaning of certain words, but this is not the case in oral storytelling (Rosen 1988). Gestures, facial expression, intonation, repetition of phrases all contribute to making meaning accessible.

Moyles (1995) has identified three key features of storytelling

- it is a personal and individual act of imagination

- it is essentially social and participative

- it works for all age groups.

Moyles points to the valuable role that storytelling plays in the bilingual classroom by providing a natural context for the use of first languages: 'The universal qualities of story mean that cultural traditions from home and school can be brought together on an equal basis.' Thus are barriers relating to cultural and language differences broken down.

We wanted the children to believe in our tales before they went into the Enchanted Forest – so we told them stories about it, stimulating their imaginations and making them believe in the magical elements in it. When we told story about the dog getting lost in the Forest, we used a common name for dogs in Pakistan – Kaliya. The children were led to believe that the jinns had taken Kaliya and that they were the ones setting the tasks. This undoubtedly heightened the children's experiences and added to their excitement.

Beard (1984) has argued that the spoken word 'acts as a kind of seed bed from which writing skills can grow', and Dixon and Stratta (1986) have provided evidence that children in the early stages of writing conform to an oral mode and gradually develop a more appropriate written mode. Both arguments endorse the importance of oral language on written tasks. It is also argued that telling stories builds up confidence and enhances oracy and that this in turn benefits literacy. It is important that we do not underestimate the complex demands of the writing process and view each piece of work as unique and individual.

I decided to explore my hypothesis that oral storytelling affects story writing within the imaginative context of the Enchanted Forest. Do children adopt ideas from oral stories when they are writing stories? I elected to work with a group of seven children, three boys and four girls. They were informed about the nature of my research and were enthusiastic to co-operate.

Stories were used to excite the children's imagination and belief in the magic and fantasy elements of the Forest. These stories had some of the elements of fairy tales and some similarity of events, character and plot, in, for instance, 'Jack and the Beanstalk', 'Hansel and Gretel' and 'Aladdin'. The stories were modified to reflect the children's cultural backgrounds and experiences and references were made to the jinns. Characters had Asian names and familiar cultural vocabulary such as 'open sim sim' instead of 'open sesame'. Telling stories in the children's first language made it easier for them to understand connotations and meanings.

The children were told that they would be writing imaginative stories over the next few sessions in the Enchanted Forest. Children need a clear purpose for their writing and I decided that the stories could be used to make a book we could put in the classroom for the staff and children to read. The children wrote their stories inside the Enchanted Forest and the setting motivated them. Several chose to write sitting on the floor and using clipboards for support. Their stories were first drafted orally, allowing them to tell the whole group what they were going to write about. Then they discussed and formatted their stories in pairs – inventing, planning, working out and redrafting. They composed plots, described characters, resolved problems and derived conclusions. They also chose the title for their story. Once they were satisfied with their oral compositions, they wrote their stories. In the next session the children read the stories aloud to the whole group, who offered positive helpful comments and appreciation, that gave all concerned a sense of fulfilment. We followed this pattern of working several more times, always beginning with their working collaboratively in groups to think of ideas about what the story would be about, draft their stories orally and then start to write them down on paper. In subsequent sessions the children could finish their stories and compose and write still more.

Through listening to story, children begin to intuitively acquire a knowledge of story structures and to gain familiarity with grammatical features. They develop story grammars and a 'knowledge of formal vocabulary and style which characterise forms of writing' (Bean and Wagstaff, 1991). They begin to understand how the narrative style operates – how the elements of character, plot, action and setting work together to create a story. They become well versed in the style, structure and vocabulary required of story writing through their encounters with stories and this enables them to verbalise and write imaginative fiction fluently.

Written stories differ significantly from oral stories, although the conventions of beginnings and endings, such as 'once upon a time' and 'happily ever after' are evident in both (Meek, 1991). To write their own stories, children need a subject and a wealth of words and structures with which to express their ideas, and they gain this from past experience, through hearing, reading, watching or dramatising (Dixon and Stratta, 1986).

I used several methods to analyse the children's written stories. Labov's (1972) investigations of oral storytelling have contributed significantly to the analysis of narrative discourse and I drew on his features of orientation, complicating action, evaluation and resolution, examining the use of character, setting and time, happenings, the narrator's role and the outcome of events. I considered long complex sentences in comparison to short sentences, the range of adjectives used and, most importantly, the cohesiveness of the text. I also evaluated how the children introduced characters, plot, setting and style as suggested by Bean and Wagstaff (1991) to determine children's awareness of the elements they required to write stories.

I analysed samples of writing from the seven children involved in my research. The impact of our storytelling in the Enchanted Forest is reflected in these stories composed by two of the children – Sajid and Abdullah. Both children struggle with the writing process.

The spooky casel *by Sajid*

Once up on a time not to long ago in the days of mist there lived there was a little girl cald mis bassi. She decided to tell her dad the scietst to disin her a time machen hare dady worked so hard he worked day and night for 10 hol months soon the time machen was finished the nws was spredid all around the world there was a nother time machen and it was cald the scientific time machen the one that the scientist made was the scraps of the hanfit time machen so Mrs basey took the time machen to the en chanted Forest and she prest the wrong button and the jin came back so thats wht the enchanted Forest is haunted and Kaliya has vanishd into thine air and it is scary.

Sajid begins his story with 'Once upon a time' and indeed begins all his stories thus! He embellishes it with 'not too long ago in the days of mist' clearly something he has adopted from his knowledge of stories and story conventions. His teacher, Maggie, made a point of using different openings to stories. Sajid continues with descriptive fairytale prose using phrases such as 'worked day and night,' 'ten whole months,' 'spread all over the world,' 'vanished into thin air.' He has actually produced a narrative that provides the reason for the Forest's creation.

The title of Sajid's story bears little relevance to the text. Perhaps the context of the Enchanted Forest inspired this initial idea, but he then took a totally different slant. The initial story of Kaliya stimulates his thinking, then his own ideas develop and the plot is constructed in true story telling fashion. We see a range of cohesive ties within his text: 'she decided to tell her dad the scientist' demonstrated the use of an anaphoric cohesive tie (Chapman, 1987 cited in Tann, 1991) and additionally, he applies the additive 'and' and the causal connective 'so' sparingly in his text to enhance the flow. He also has a good understanding of pronouns, which he uses appropriately referring to the characters as 'he' (line 4) and 'she' (line 2 and 10) to sustain the thread of the story. His complicated sentences inspire the reader to continue reading. Throughout his story, Sajid uses orientations and actions in order to set the scene and keep the reader informed.

Sajid spoke constantly about his desire to be a scientist. He recounted stories read and told to him by his older brother who had a fascination with science. 'My brother tells me stories, but he doesn't read them from a book. They are really good stories'. He demonstrated great expertise in solving the scientific aspects of the clues set in the Forest, using scientific vocabulary in context, and was the first child to apply the words 'conductor' and 'reflector' in his experimentation. He was extremely articulate about the experiential scientific tasks, but found literacy-based tasks difficult and arduous. He participated in oral storytelling with imagination, vivacity and enthusiasm, using gesture and expression to great effect. He listens to stories with interest, absorbing ideas and new vocabulary which he uses in his written work. Within this narrative, he selects and shapes language in order to bring to life his experiences and his ambition to be a scientist and I feel that he identifies himself with the 'scientist' in his story.

But writing appears to be an arduous task for Sajid, as indicated by some illegible writing in his text. He is conscious of his capabilities and the difficulties he encounters in literacy but contributed valuable comments to the discussions about writing and the processes involved. He recognises the importance of listening to stories in relation to writing your own –

> 'She could not make stories up because she would not know what a story is without listening to lots first.'

'You can learn a lot of new words in the brain when you listen to interesting stories. You can also learn lots of stories and you can tell them to other people.'

Sajid frequently responded to his writing in a very negative way: 'I wish I had writing like you;' 'no-one likes my writing;' 'my spelling is no good,' 'you are the only one who can read my writing'. Yet when his oral responses and participation are examined it is obvious that he is extremely articulate as well as being alert to metalinguistic processes. He needs to realise that he has good understanding of the structure of story, that he uses adjectival and adverbial phrases to good effect and that his narrative is cohesive and fluent.

The magic tree and 30 thieves *by Abdullah*
One spooky night there lived a boy called Matloob he got sucked up a tree.

Up the tree there was all scary jinns and a castl made out gold.

Miss Bassi came in a room Miss Bassi got cross she said give me my dog.

The jinn said find the magic key

She said haw can I find the key She fond the key and she fond the door the jinn came out of the tree The jinn got happy and the dog got friy at last

The End

Abdullah began his story with a traditional story phrase: 'one spooky night', which he presumably also derived from the telling of Hansel and Gretel. He introduces a character named Matloob, but then abandons him and continues with a new character – Miss Bassi. This has an obvious effect on the overall cohesion of the story. The title is not directly related to his story except for the tree. Any connections have to be made implicitly by the reader. Abdullah needs to gain an awareness of audience.

The use of the phrase 'sucked up the tree' is directly evolved from the story Sara Ali told during the problem-solving in the Forest, when she accounted for her disappearance. He has borrowed several elements from other stories told in the Forest – the jinns, the magic key, the lost dog, the castle of gold. His narrative appears to be rather elliptical and he leaves a substantial gap after his first sentence which isolates it from the rest of the text and affects the sequence of the story, creating a lack of cohesion. He omits details which would have given clarity. Through discussions Abdullah could be encouraged to think about elaborations such as how Miss Bassi found the key, why the jinn was happy or the relevance of the castle of gold. He used an additive 'and' twice, but normally opted for repetition rather than connectives to give cohesion to his text. His use of connectives should be developed in his telling and writing of stories

Abdullah needed to know how to introduce characters properly. He could have added to the story's climax by making more of the excitement of finding Kaliya. He provided a summary of events but needs to develop his writing through elaborating his characters and events.

Abdullah's reading age is three years below his chronological age but he enjoys stories, particularly those that relate directly to his personal ex-

The Castle of Gold

perience. His parents occasionally tell him stories at home and he commented on stories that he had watched on the news. He said that he enjoyed telling stories in Panjabi and listening to the stories about the Enchanted Forest. His class teacher remarked on his motivation and self-esteem, which had improved considerably since the beginning of the school year. He grasps new concepts quickly but struggles with literacy, particularly with writing down his ideas. He needs to improve the structure and conventions of his writing.

It was evident from the children's stories that they were influenced by the stories previously told to them, echoing the events, characters and plots. Although the children introduced their characters in various ways, describing their actions or appearance, detail was very limited. Readers who, for example, do not share the same cultural background will not understand the references to jinns and will be left to build pictures for themselves. Similarly the children seem to assume that listeners or readers know as much as they do about the story content. Sajid, however, shows his awareness of audience, introducing his characters appropriately: 'Miss Bassi is a scientist's daughter'. Calkins (1986) and Graves (1983) have both noted that between the ages of 7 and 9, children begin to become fluent story writers and their awareness of audience increases.

Our two 'model' storytellers, Sajid and Abdullah, indicated in the interviews that they are confident in participating in group discussions. They enjoyed the work in the Forest and understand the relevance of story and the processes involved in composition. My work with the children convinced me that if we did more to build children's storytelling skills their story writing would improve.

I decided to collect further data through three group interviews, largely unstructured to allow for free discussion. The first explored the children's ideas about what they thought helped them to write stories. Open ended questions facilitated the informality and the children spoke spontaneously. Tape recording the interviews seemed to imbue them with a real sense of importance. The following illustrate the children's views on story writing.

Lakhbir	What do you think of when you are writing a story?
Abdullah	I think of what will happen in my story.
Sajid	Yeah, that's right, such as what will happen and what you will imagine will happen.
Ahmed	And there are times when miss tells us a story. We then remember it and write it in our own stories, like we remember the dog Kaliya that got lost in the Forest.

Abdullah	I don't like writing but I like to make my own stories up.
Sajid	I like writing them. I like to make stories up. Sometimes it is hard to remember stories that you have heard.
Saleha	I like writing stories but don't like to read my own. I think other people's stories are better. Like if I wrote a story I wouldn't like it, but If someone like Samina wrote a story, then I would like it.
Asiah	But you write good stories, I like them.
Abdullah	We need to listen to lots of stories to help us write our own stories.
Asiah	Stories put ideas into our heads and knowledge so we can write our own stories.
Saleha	I like to listen to stories.
Samina	If we didn't listen to stories, we wouldn't know what to write. 'Once upon a time' is something I learned from stories.
Asiah	I think stories are important for my writing.

During the second interview we discussed their experiences in the Enchanted Forest, reflecting on what they had enjoyed doing and what aspects of the stories they could remember. We also discussed the children's views and opinions on stories read and stories told, both in school and at home.

Lakhbir	Do you all prefer to read stories or tell them?
All	Tell them.
Sajid	When you are reading it, you begin to get bored. Your eyes start hurting and you get tired.
Abdullah	It can make you go to sleep.
Ahmed	It takes time to read stories and you might get stuck on a word you don't know. If you tell a story it can be what you like. You can make the story up.
Lakhbir	Do you like to hear stories that are read or told?
Abdullah	I like to hear them and read them, so that you can tell them to other people.
Samina	In some ways it's better to read a story in a book, because you can read it again and again.
Asiah	You might forget what to say when you are telling a story, but you can't with a book. It has more details.
Sajid	My brother tells me stories, but he doesn't read them from a book. They are really good stories.
Samina	I like the stories about the Enchanted Forest.
Sajid	You can learn a lot of new words in the brain when you listen to interesting stories. You can also learn lots of stories and you can tell them to other people.

Asiah	I find stories that are read and told interesting and really nice.
Lakhbir	Does anyone read stories to you at home?
Asiah	My mom, my dad tells me lots of different stories.
Ahmed	I listen to stories in Urdu from my mom.
Abdullah	I heard a story on the news about a boy that got into trouble by the police.
Saleha	My sister tells me stories but she always reads Pocahontas.
Samina	My dad tells me funny stories and stories about India, where the temples are. Miss like the one on this picture. (Points to my key ring).
Amina	I told my friends about Kaliya and how he got lost in the Forest, and it was magic when we found him.
Abdullah	I had a dream of the story of the Enchanted Forest. There were crocodiles, they were real.

It was important to acknowledge that children had experiences of story in their homes. The stories may not be in written form to be read to them, but nevertheless children have extensive and diverse experience of story from their oral culture, television and video.

The last interview in my data collection gave me useful insights into children's attitudes and experiences of story at home and school and into their thoughts and feelings on the issue of story. I was interested in the children's views on story and story writing, looking for evidence to suggest that oral stories enhances their writing.

Lakhbir	What do you all think of the stories that you have written for me?
Abdullah	It's been very exciting, because we have written stories about the Enchanted Forest.
Sajid	Yeah, it's been real fun.
Ahmed	Scary as well.
Sajid	We learn lots of things when we listen to stories, language, knowledge and new words.
Asiah	And how to read a book.
Samina	I don't like my stories.
Lakhbir	Why not?
Samina	Because I wrote them. If anyone else wrote a story, I would like it.
Amina	We like your stories.
Samina	That's because you have not written it, that's why you like it.

Lakhbir	Does that mean that if Amina wrote a story she would not like it, but everyone else will?
Samina	Yes.
Asiah	That's not true.
Sajid	I am not happy with my stories, because sometimes I can't read my writing.
Lakhbir	I can read it.
Asiah	It's just because your writing is scruffy. You can improve your writing just like I did. My writing used to be scruffy.
Sajid	My spelling is always wrong.
Abdullah	You can get help for your spelling, ask Miss Bassi or use a dictionary.
Lakhbir	Have the stories that we have told you helped you to write your own stories?
Asiah	Yes, it has helped me a lot.
Lakhbir	How?
Asiah	Because if we did not know anything about the Forest, then how could we write about it?
Samina	It has helped us to write stories in the Forest because we can see everything.
Sajid	The Enchanted Forest helps you to make your own stories up. There are lots of ideas you can get just from looking.
Asiah	It is a magic Forest. It helps us to imagine. It has helped us to be in the Forest. If we could not see it then we could not imagine anything.

(The children read their stories aloud to each other.)

Lakhbir	Are you all happy with your stories?
Asiah	I like my story 'Jinn of the Jinn Land,' because it has good words. The Forest helped me.
Samina	My story is a bit boring about the green spooky tunnel.
Amina	I like that story, the picture is good as well.
Saleha	My writing can improve a bit, but I've enjoyed writing my stories.
Abdullah	Miss, the story you told us helped.
Ahmed	That's like me, I got my ideas for one of the stories that Miss Ali told us, the one about the monkey and the jinn.
Sajid	I like my stories a bit, I have not got good spelling. I don't think that my writing will improve.
Lakhbir	I am sure that you can be like me, your writing will improve just like mine did.
Sajid	Miss, if you wasn't here I couldn't write a good story. You and the Enchanted Forest have helped me a lot. I can write six pages.
Abdullah	Miss, can we do it all again?

Stars in the dark

One day it was very dark and there was a storme. There was a dog called Khalia. He had a friend called Aladdin and Aladdin had a brother called Jony. One day when everybody was a sleep when the magic stars was out Khalia went outside and the stars took him to the Jini's land. They tied him in the bedroom and this bedroom was magic. When Aladdin came from school and Jony went out side but the stars did not work in the morning so in the night they went but still it did not work because they needed an animal. One day they brought a mouse and they went into the jini's land and they went to the bedroom and they found Khalia they quickly went before the jinis saw them and they never went out again when the stars are out. They lived happly ever after.

bewear of the stars

it might happen to you?

The un of the un land

One day we went to the Enchanted Forest. There were some visitors from the land of the jin. They set out a task for us to do. The jinns looked very very scary. They were all over the Enchanted Forest, but there was still some bufterflles and bufferfly plants. There were crocodiles and lions, there was a dead lion as usual. There was an enchanted palace. There were loads of visitors inside the palace. They were upside down as usual. That 5 where the jInns lived. there was this river it had magic stones to get to the other side. You have to say magic words to cross to the other side. There was one that we made up it was called river deep and river wide, let me cross to the other side. Then I saw a tunnel that was long and It had wiggly lines. I saw a cave the cave had lots of creatures. The enchanted forest looks very scary. It looks like it never happened before. There are lots of wicked things I saw.

> ### The Enchanted forest
> Once up in a time we came to the Enchanted Forest to rescue Kaliya. We had to find some clues. The jinn put the clues all over the enchanted forest. When we found all 5 clues. We had to make a parcel so we had to find the key. It was under the pineapple when found it said on the clue that you had to protect the key if in case. There was a thunder that day was Tuesday 25th February. We nearly made the parcel but we didn't have times we had to go. If we didn't go we couldn't find Kaliya but we were sfill half way through the parcel. I'm sorry Kaliya we couldn't free you
>
> From your friend

The experiences of working in the context of the Enchanted Forest inspire me to create an atmosphere in my future classroom where stories will flow and become a major means of learning, enjoyment and developing children's power over language. Using the imaginative context of the Forest for telling stories provided an excellent stimulus for children to write. As Rosen (1988) observes: 'Teaching and learning can never change without a special kind of imaginative act, which all the curriculum guides in the world cannot render unnecessary'. Oral storytelling can extend children's knowledge of stories that come from a wide range of cultures as well as affirming cultural diversity.

This research has highlighted further points of interest. Firstly storytelling gives opportunities for children to develop their own ideas, using their own voices, gaining a sense of their own power. Secondly children develop as effective writers in relation to what they hear – although not only through storytelling. Story is also experienced through the media, reading, anecdotes and the range of different experiences gained from cultural and personal and language diversity.

Thirdly there is a danger that we, as teachers, will respond to children's written stories by looking at their handwriting, spelling and punctuation without giving due consideration to the content. This study has shown that children – like Sajid – whose work appears untidy and poorly spelt can have 'such strengths as varied phrase structure, thematic variety, appropriate style lying beneath the unpromising surface' (Perera, 1984). Every child's story is in some way unique. However, this uniqueness is only recognised if we look beyond the surface features.

The green spooky tunnel

One day there was a boy called Aladdin and he had a dog called Kaliya. He was missing in the forest. This forest was enchanted and one day Aladdin went to the forest and started to find Kaiiya. And Kallya was stuck in the tunnel. And Aladdin could not go there because he was in a cave. The Jinni came and Aladdin was hiding and the jinni said do you want to come out. It was the baby jinni he was a friendly jinni and he did not see Aladdin and he freed Kaliya. He went to his land and Aladdin got Kaliya and went home. The big jinni wanted Khalia for dinner and he was very cross. And the baby jinni started laughing. One day the dog went into a forest and Aladdin was at school and Khalia was in the spooky green tunnel. And when Aladdin came from school he said where is Khalia and he looked in the tunnel and the baby jinni freed Khalia and Aladdin took him home. And the baby jinni said where is Khalia to the big jinni and Khalia was not there and the big jinni died. The liftie jinni was laughing and everybody lived happily ever after.

The End.

The Magic Carpet

One day there was a magic carpet that was the jinni's carpet if you go on the carpet the jini will get you on his land. I was so scared. On day I went to the enchanted forest. I saw the magic carpet. I got stuck. I was flying, flying and flying the carpet stopped. I flew down and then I went back to my house. I told my mum what happened. From that day I was scared. One day I went to school and the students came in and took me to the enchanted forest. They said to me to go and find the key. So I did I saw the key and got it. I opened the door. Kaliya came out. I was so happy to see Kaliya. The jinns went away to their house and they never came again.

Thank you

From Tahira

The effect of oral storytelling on children's writing should not be under-estimated. It can provide stimulus and motivation and bring an interesting edge to their work. Wherever possible, teachers should seek to capitalise on this powerful learning tool. Even the children recognised this. Their responses were brilliant.

The magic lamp

One dark dark night there was a lamp. It was made of gold. And I found the lamp from the magic door. And the lamp had lots of magic powers.One day the lamp got stuck in the magic door and It couldn t get out. One day a girl came with some magic powers. Nobody can see only the lamp can see her. She had lost her dog and she wanted the jinn to help her find the dog but the jinn did not help her. She turned the jinn into a monkey. At last she found the dog. The dog was so so hungry and then she found the dog and gave the dog some food.

The End

The Enchanted Forest

One spooky night when we came to the Enchanted Forest we had to find the clues and they told us what to do. A boy called Haider dropped the castle down and we were so scared that the jinn got us. And then we had to find the key. The key was magic. The key was waterproof, but if we put the key in the water then the magic would go away and Kaliya won't be freed. He is lost in the forest and the jinns got Kaliya in their house. He is afraid of the jinns and he is very hungry.

I wish that there will be a surprise next week and that the jinn will let Kaliya free from his house.

The End

CHAPTER 7
PARTNERSHIP AND COLLABORATION: THE TEACHER'S PERSPECTIVE

MAGGIE POWER

Too often these days the individual class teacher is isolated, bombarded with paper but alone in her responsibility for a class of children's learning for a year. It's an awesome task and far more important to each individual child and family than the work of all the administrators, inspectors and other professionals involved in education. What that teacher does on a day to day basis inside that room will facilitate or restrict the progress each child will make during that year. In school there is little thinking time; every waking moment is filled with doing. All the structures and guidance offered to us from outside the classroom if anything intensifies this feeling. This project offered me time to think and reflect on what is important for children. The financial cost was minimal. The richness came from the excitement of the students and lecturers and the expertise they brought with them.

To have the chance to bring in other motivated and interested adults to work alongside the children and teacher is a rare gift. Collaborating with the college allowed me to offer more to the children in my care and they benefited from the additional input. They could listen to their first language being used in the classroom and see it being valued by me. They could engage in challenging and stimulating interaction in small groups. They had the benefit of working in an environment that I would have had neither the time nor expertise to create. They had the opportunity to work on tasks devised by a specialist science teacher educator, which I am not. But above all they were challenged within the context of a good story and they enjoyed it.

The first morning visitors arrived in my classroom was unforgettable. The sustained interest, excitement and work that started that day made it a joy to be part of the activities. The students had a good story that all could share. As they switched from English to Panjabi, there was a gasp that indicated amazed interest. Some children turned towards me – What would I do? How would I respond? I listened and waited until there was an opportunity to ask the class to share what they had listened to with me. Immediately the balance changed: I needed their language skills to open doors for me – to introduce me to the story section that I had been unable to understand.

Then it was time to ask for volunteers. Every child wanted to be in the first group to go into the Forest though they had no idea yet about where it was. The hardest thing for me was to be denied the opportunity to see their faces when they entered the Forest. I had seen it grow behind closed doors. I knew they would be excited and astounded to find such a magical space in school and yet I had to stay in my room with the class, just letting the children go in small groups with the students.

One child, Shereen, said later, 'First I thought I was scared but when I went inside it was not scary'. And Saleha told me, 'We felt scared, we thought our friends wouldn't come back'. I had agreed to maintain the suspense and excitement. Saleha kept a list of the names of the children who left the room. We discussed where they might have gone to.

As each group went and didn't return, the suspense rose. As the end of the session approached I could feel the tension in the air and one child announced apprehensively that she did not want to go in case she never came back. After some discussion it was decided that I would go with them because, as we all agreed, it was my job to keep them all safe.

As I shut my classroom door with the last group of children, all of us wearing our protective cloaks, I knew we would all be hooked, all of us willing and eager to work within the context of the story for the duration of the project – and that everyone would benefit.

The Forest became the stimulus for the rest of the week's work. Children focused on other work because I'm afraid I declared that only those who worked very hard all week would be able to go into it. We needed hard workers and good brains to find the dog. One child in particular, who was difficult to stimulate and sometimes unable to concentrate and work to his potential, became engaged as never before in school work for fear of missing a journey to the Forest. Others checked that it wasn't a Forest day before letting parents arrange dental appointments. Attendance at our school is good but on Forest days it was excellent.

The children were also able to focus on other work at different times. They remained excited and enthusiastic about the project, but were able to concentrate on other areas of the curriculum and not be distracted for the rest of the time. They couldn't contain themselves when they returned from each Forest visit – they had so much to share and communicate. At times it was nearly overwhelming; even the quietest of children was bursting to tell what they had done, found out, heard and seen. After each visit, they wanted to tell me what the clues were, what they had had to make and find. They were willing to miss playtime to talk about it all.

The children were also rewarded. As if finding a real dog were not enough, each child was presented with a certificate that acknowledged their hard work in rescuing Kaliya. These certificates were proudly taken home and given a special place on many a Bradford mantelpiece. The parents and families also became intrigued and one afternoon after school we opened the Forest to families, who much enjoyed looking around. They had the chance to examine the clues and to discuss with us the learning opportunities made possible for the children by such a way of working.

The Forest offered every child the chance to think and to do, to be engaged in creative and developmental thinking that involved drawing upon past learning and then applying it to a practical situation. The look on children's faces when they are engaged in thinking, searching for solutions, is what teaching is all about.

For the adults involved it was a creative and stimulating time, made possible by our link with the college. Such links, built up and extended over the years, have allowed for mutual development and growth. The students have brought fresh ideas and initiatives and the children in school have benefited from the interaction and stimulus provided by the many adults involved.

The environment constructed has been provided at minimal cost and has become a rich resource that others in Bradford can access and use. Links with college outside of the conventional teaching practice situation in which students are examined have proved advantageous to all concerned. The students can try things out and practise with the children and the children can be supported and challenged by the contact with a new lot of adults who provide stimulation and learning opportunities. This is something I would recommend other schools to do. Links between institutions also enable the teachers to step outside of their day to day situation and spend time reflecting. As others work with and look at your class you can be enlightened by what they perceive and the talents they can develop in your children.

The Head teacher of Grange Road First School, Mrs Passey, described the project as invaluable and the benefits to individual children as immeasurable. She said, 'It was obvious to anyone watching that the children greeted the language students eagerly and that they had hardly set foot inside the classroom door when they were bombarded with questions'. The children expected to be engaged in detailed conversation about an adventure they were all sharing. It wasn't a teacher/pupil situation but one of let's-go-on-this-adventure-together. They shared the adventure of problem-solving.

The children were stretched in terms of their language development and forced into a situation where they had to draw on prior knowledge, to share language skills, first to understand and then to act on the clues. Children with the confidence to translate did so and could be seen to be negotiating meaning with others in their group. One boy, Ilyas, took on the role of ensuring other children's understanding when interpreting and acting upon clues.

The children demonstrated their capacity to retain the knowledge and share it later with members of the school and their families and friends. It was genuine communication with a purpose. Above all it was focused. I knew I could look at the videos of them working, but I was not there while they interacted, so if they wanted me to know they had to explain and talk until they were satisfied that I understood what they had seen, read about, listened to and finally achieved.

They hugely enjoyed entering the magic world of the Forest – as they wrote in the class poem, they were stepping into timeless days where they were free from worries. They became absorbed with the story and collectively sustained belief in it. As the weeks passed they gave it continued credibility by the questions they asked and the roles they maintained for themselves. They accepted that completing the tasks could lead to the discovery of the missing dog. They accepted the story set in Pakistan and stepped into it in the middle of Bradford – and it worked for us all. They took the story home with them and shared it with others, families and friends, and they brought back other stories of forests and jinns to share in school.

In relation to the science they had the space to return to areas covered previously in the curriculum, knowledge they needed to solve the clues. The knowledge and information they had already acquired had a purpose. Most groups succeeded also because they were able to share their knowledge and listen to each other. In some cases the child least expected was the one who took the lead role.

A year later I took some time to talk to many of the children who had worked in the Enchanted Forest. Twenty three of the twenty eight who had left our school had moved to the same nearby middle school. They spent an hour and a half with me remembering, answering questions and generally enjoying the time to chat and recall, what had been fun learning for them all. We looked at pictures I had brought and I asked them whether they would help me by writing the answers to some questions about the Forest, even though it was a year later, and to tell me what they thought each of the words from the clues that I had listed meant. While they were doing this I asked particular children to chat to me and share their thoughts about the work they had done in the Forest.

These were the questions I asked them one year on:

What was the story you were told before you went into the Forest?

How was that story told to you?

Who were you looking for?

What did you have to do when you were in the Forest?

Can you remember the magic words you had to say before you crossed the water?

Did you work on your own or in a group when you were in the Forest?

What sort of work did you have to do?

What did you have to make in the Forest?

If you had to do it again how would you do it?

Would you like to go again if there was another forest near you?

Have you still got your certificate?

Would you like to say anything else about the work in 4P when you went into the Forest?

It was a delightful session. It is always good to see old friends! They remembered the sounds and colours, and they recalled feeling frightened but then realising it was more interesting than frightening. Sajid talked about having to use all his senses. They all remembered that the story had been about finding the lost dog and could recall the lines, 'River deep, river wide let me cross to the other side'. Only one child changed it slightly and wrote, 'River white let me cross to the other side'. They talked about how excited they had been when the dog appeared.

117

Others told me how they knew the room was changed, how paper was put over the windows and trees were hung down from the ceiling. It had been our Forest and yet a year on they were able to see it as something that was constructed and could – indeed should – now be shared with other schools. One child suggested they could have our Forest or they could make their own. Yet while it was there and when they entered into it it was real, challenging to work in and worth remembering.

This says something about the value of poetry and story as instruments of instruction, as vehicles through which to teach. The children knew it was made of paper. If you asked them they could tell you that the river that flowed through the room was a blue cloth, yet their imaginations also enabled them to accept it as a river that you needed magic words to cross safely. A good storyteller can use children's imaginations to educate rather than instruct and, as the advert says, you never forget a good teacher.

The children could also remember making a bridge and a boat and having to devise something waterproof. Fewer children wrote about the circuit, which surprised me as it had been one of their most successful and exciting tasks. These were tangible outcomes, products they could name a whole year later. This contrasted well with the end of the session when one of them showed me a science work book on Light and Sound. I said that should be easy, as we did those topics in the summer term last year when I had taught them. But they weren't sure; they could remember the science of the Forest but not the end of term's work! I would see that as a comment on the story context rather than on formal instruction about sound and light!

All but four children still had their certificates and one boy was keen to tell me that I owed him one because he had been away in Pakistan when they were presented at the end of the year and had not been back to his old school since. One child said it was in their house but she did not know where as her dad was keeping it somewhere special.

In answer to the question: How was the story told to you? seventeen of the children made particular reference to their pleasure at the story being told to them in more that one language. They also remembered the students' names and that one of them had been sucked up a tree – an interesting way of explaining a colleague's absence on a Monday morning.

All remembered solving the problems and knew that the work involved had been science based. Shaheen said that they had done work on electricity in science at her new school. She had worked on how to make a switch and a circuit and said that while doing so she had thought about the Forest. She went on to say, 'I think all the schools in England should have a forest in their school because they will enjoy it. The certificate I got, I have still got it. I would like to go again'. All the children contacted would like to return to the Forest and do all the tasks again.

Taking the children into a creative space and offering them challenges that required them to recall and apply their scientific knowledge had clearly been both memorable and of educational value to both children and students. The children benefited from working collaboratively in negotiating meaning for the clues provided. They shared and pooled information in pursuit of a common goal. The adults worked alongside the children, using their first language at times, and supporting them as thinkers rather than providing them with answers. There was a feeling throughout that the experience was shared and that the children could bring into the Forest all of their language skills and be valued for them. They were sustained by their enjoyment and motivated to work for the rest of the week.

It was learning,

it was demanding,

it was language work,

it was science work,

it was sharing,

it was negotiating,

but most of all,

it was **fun!**

REFERENCES

Ambrus, V. (1992) Never laugh at bears. Penguin

Armitage, M. (1998) Playground culture. The state of play, perspectives of children's oral culture (April 1998) National Centre for English Cultural Tradition

Baker, C. (1993) Foundations of bilingual education and bilingualism. Multilingual Matters

Barnes, D. (1976) From communication to curriculum. Penguin

Barnes, D. and Todd F. (1977) Communication and learning in small groups. Routledge

Beard, R. (1984) Children's writing in the primary school. Hodder and Stoughton

Bean, M. A. and Wagstaff, P. (1991) Practical approaches to writing in the primary school. Longman

Bennett, N. (1976) Teaching styles and pupil progress. Open Books

Bennett, N. and Dunne, E. (1990) Talking and learning in groups. MacMillan

Blackledge, A. (ed) (1994) Teaching bilingual children. Trentham

Brock, A. (1998) 'Into the Enchanted Forest' in Dziecko W Swiecie przyrodyinauki. Children in the world of nature and science. Torún-Poznan

Bruce, T. (1987) Early childhood education. Hodder and Stoughton

Calkins, S. (1986) The art of teaching writing. Heinemann

Campbell, R. and Miller.L. (1995) Supporting children in the early years. Trentham

Carter, R. (1990) (ed) Knowledge about language and the curriculum – LINC reader. Hodder and Stoughton

Cramer, I. (1997) in Gregory, E. (ed) One child, many worlds. David Fulton

Clarke, J. and Goods, T (1996) Drama Volume No. 4

Cummins, J. (1984) Bilingualism and special educational: Issues in assessment. Multilingual Matters

Cummins J and Swain (1986) Bilingualism in education: Aspects of theory, research and practice Multilingual Matters

DES (Department of Education and Science) Plowden Report (1967) Children and their primary schools; A report of the Central Advisory Council. Volume 1. HMSO

DES (1988) National Curriculum proposals for English for ages 5 to 11 (The Cox Committee Report) HMSO

DES (1990) English in the National Curriculum. DES

DES (1995) Dearing in the National Curriculum. HMSO

DES (1975) Bullock Report: A language for life. HMSO

DfE (Department for Education) (1995) Key Stages 1 and 2 of the National Curriculum. HMSO

DfE (1995) Science in the National Curriculum HMSO

DfEE (Department for Education and Employment) (1995) National Curriculum Key Stages 1 and 2. HMSO

DfEE (1997a) Requirements for Courses of Initial Teacher Training Circular 10/97. DfEE

DfEE (1997b) The implementation of the National Literacy Strategy. DfEE

Dixon, J and Stratta, L. (1986) Writing narrative and beyond. The Canadian Council of Teachers of English

Donaldson, M. (1978) Children's minds. Collins Fontana

Dougill, P. and Knott, R. (1988) The primary language book. Open University Press

Edwards, A. D. and Westgate, D.P.G. (1994) Investigating classroom talk. (2nd edition) Falmer Press

Edwards, D. and Mercer, N. (1987) Common knowledge: the development of knowledge and understanding in the classroom. Methuen

Fisher, R. (1990) Teaching children to think. Blackwell

Fisher, R. (1995) Teaching children to learn. Stanley Thornes

Fitzpatrick, F. (1987) The Open door: the Bradford bilingual project. Multilingual Matters

Fitzpatrick, F. (1994) The linguistic background to ESL. BICC

Fox, C. (1993) At the very edge of the forest; The influence of literature on storytelling by young children. Cassell

Fox, C. (1995) in Campbell and Miller Supporting children in the early years. Trentham

Goodman, K. (1991) What's whole in whole language? Scholastic Educational

Graves, D. (1983) Writing: teachers and children's work. Heinemann

Gregory, E. (1997) (ed) One child, many worlds. David Fulton

Gross, D. (1992) Psychology the science of mind and behaviour. Hodder and Stoughton

Grugeon, E; Hubbard, L; Smith, C; and Dawes, L (1998) Teaching speaking and listening in the primary school. David Fulton

Hall, D. (1995) Assessing the needs of bilingual children living in two languages. David Fulton

Halliday, M.A.K. (1978) Language as social semiotic; the social interpretation of language and meaning. Arnold

Harlen, W. (1993) Teaching and learning primary science Paul Chapman

Heath, S.B. (1983) Ways with words: Language, life and work in communities and classrooms. Cambridge University Press

Heath, S.B. (1994) in Maybin J. (ed.) (1994) Language and literacy in social practice. Multilingual Matters

Heathcote, D. and Bolton, G. (1995) Drama for learning. Heinemann

Hislam in Moyles J. (1996) Children learning through play. Open University Press

Johnston, J. (1996) Early explorations in science. Open University Press

Jones, A. and Buttrey, J (1970) Children and stories. Basil Blackwell

Labov, W. (1972) Language in the inner city. Blackwell

Luke, A. and Kale, J. (1997) in Gregory (1997) One child, many worlds. David Fulton

McCarthy, M. (1991) Discourse analysis for teachers. Cambridge University Press

McCarthy, M. (1994) Language as discourse; perspectives for language teaching. Longman

McWilliam, N. (1996) The importance of connotative discourse in teacher education for multilingual contexts. BICC

McWilliam, N. (1998) What's in a word? vocabulary development in multilingual classrooms. Trentham

Meek, M. (1991) On being literate. The Bodley Head Children's Books

Mercer, N. (1987) Common knowledge; the development of understanding in the classroom. Methuen

Moyles, J. (1995) Beginning teaching; beginning learning in primary education. Open University Press

Moyles, J. (1996) Children learning through play. Open University Press

Neelands, J. (1984) Making sense of drama. A guide to classroom practice. Heinemann.

Neelands, J. (I 992) Learning through imagined experience. Hodder and Stoughton

Norman, K. (ed) (1992) Thinking voices: the work of the National Oracy Project. Hodder and Stoughton

Ollerenshaw, C. and Ritchie, R. (1997) Primary science – making it work. David Fulton

O'Neill, C. et al (1990) Drama structures for teachers – a professional handbook for teachers. Stanley Thornes

Osborne, R. and Freyberg, P. (1985) Learning in science: the implications of children's science Heinemann

Paley, V.G. (198I) Wally's stories. Harvard University Press

Perera, K. (1984) Children's writing and reading; analysing classroom language. Blackwell

Pinsent, P. (1992) Language, culture and young children. David Fulton

Pollard, A. and Tann, S. (1993) Reflective teaching in the primary school. Cassell

Readman, G. and Lamont, G. (1996) Drama: a handbook for primary teachers. BBC Educational

Romaine, S. (1991) Bilingualism. Blackwell

Rosen, B. (1988) And none of it was nonsense: The power of storytelling in school. Mary Glasgow Publications

Rosen, H. (1984) Stories and meanings. NATE Publications

SCAA (1996) Key Stage One English Tasks – Reading and Writing; Teacher's Handbook. DfEE.

Sherrington, R. (1993) The ASE pimary science teachers' handbook. Simon and Schuster

Stibbs, A. (1991) Reading narrative as literature: signs of life. Open University Press

Skutnaab-Kangas, T. (1981) Bilingualism or not. Multilingual Matters

Sutton, C. (1992) Words, science and learning Open University Press

Swann Report (1985) Education for all. HMSO

Tann, S. (1991) Developing language in the primary classroom. Cassell

Tannen, 1989 in McCarthy, M. (1994) Language as discourse; perspectives for language teaching. Longman

Toolan, M.J. (1988) Narrative: a critical linguistic introduction. Routledge

Tough, J. (1976) Listening to children talking. Ward Lock Educational in association with Drake Educational Associates. Schools Council

Tough, J. (1979) Talk for teaching and learning. Ward Lock Educational

Volk, E. (ed) (1997) in Gregory, D. One child, many worlds. David Fulton

Vygotsky, L. (1962) Thought and language. Cambridge, MIT Press.

Wagner, B.J. (1976) Dorothy Heathcote: drama as a learning medium. National Education Association

Warren, K. (1992) Hooked on drama; the theory and practice of drama in early childhood. Macqarie University Institute of early childhood, Australia.

Wells, G. (1987) The meaning makers: children learning language and using language to learn. Hodder and Stoughton

Wood, D. (1988) How children think and learn. Blackwell

Woolland, B. (1993) The teaching of drama in the primary school. Longman

Wray, D. and Medwell, J. (1991) Literacy and language in the primary years. Routledge